CCAR *Journal*
A Reform Jewish Quarterly

Contents

SUSTAINING SYNAGOGUE TRANSFORMATION

LOOKING AHEAD

At the Gate – בשער

Our *machzor* Gates of Repentance instructs us (pp. 426–427): "If you wish to know the fortress to which your fathers bore their treasure, their scrolls of Torah, their Holy of Holies; if you would know the place of their deliverance; if you would find the refuge which kept your people's might spirit safe, whose age—despite the years of degradation—did not disgrace its gracious youth: If you would know all this, turn to the ancient, battered house of prayer."

The synagogue is where the soul of our people resides and from which the core of our tradition flows. It is unique in its insistence on personal moral values, its centrality to our community for prayer and study, its pastoral role in support of those in need, its trumpeting and involvement in *Tikkun Olam*, its celebration of holy Jewish time in the life of our people and sacred Jewish moments in the life of the Jew.

As the synagogue has changed and grown over the centuries, as the demands of modern life pressure us to become more than we have ever been in earlier stages of Jewish history, the need to adapt the synagogue and create new ways of reaching our people has become evident. This issue of the *CCAR Journal* is devoted to "synagogue transformation," an American Jewish attempt to reposition this ancient institution and make it increasingly more relevant in the lives of our fellow Jews. The multitude of authors and perspectives represented in these pages is testimony to both the variety and the difficulty of approaching this subject.

My deep thanks to our guest editor, Dru Greenwood, director of Synagogue Renewal at UJA-Federation in New York, and former director of the URJ's Department of Outreach. She has worked long and hard on this project, and has gathered articles representing the best that Reform Judaism has to offer on this subject. We are all the beneficiaries of her magnificent efforts.

This is my final issue as editor of the *CCAR Journal*. I want to express my deep appreciation to all those who have made the past 5½ years such a pleasure: to the CCAR staff, our publisher Mark Cohen, and my Editorial Board for their diligent reading and recommendations, to the various guest editors who have helped put together the symposia we have published, to all those who submitted articles and poetry for inclusion, and to you, the readers who make all these efforts worthwhile. The opportunity to serve in this capacity has been a singular honor for which I will be ever grateful. Under the guidance of our new editor, the Journal will continue to go from strength to strength.

Jonathan A. Stein, Editor

Synagogue Transformation:
The View from 2009

Dru Greenwood

I first encountered the language of "transformation" in something other than a scientific context in the early 1980s during the formative years of Reform Jewish outreach. It was spoken then with the intensity of new discovery in hearing the stories of *gerim* and recognizing the sacred transformation of souls, the profound change of state that was possible for individuals embracing Jewish life. What changed at that time, though, was not only the path of individual Jews-by-choice, who realized they were not alone in their quest and that their contributions might be valued, but also the families, congregations, and movement that saw the urgency for change, attended to the stories, and worked with intention over time on an uneven road toward establishing a new way of fulfilling the mitzvah of *ahavat ger*. This was a multi-level transformation, however imperfect, that, by our teacher Lawrence Hoffman's criteria for synagogue transformation explicated in this volume, led us to think differently, was pervasive and (thirty years later) long-lasting, and changed our culture. That transformation touched my life and shaped the work I am blessed to do alongside many of you. That brings us to this issue of the Journal.

Here we will look specifically at transformation of a particular institution, "synagogue transformation," its goals, methods, multiple pathways, and future possibilities. What kind of *kehillot* do we aspire to create? How can we get there—and when will we arrive? What are the pitfalls to avoid and what will be the challenges over the horizon? What leadership resources do we need to move our people toward the goal? On the one hand, these are practical questions asked and answered by every generation of Jewish leaders

DRU GREENWOOD is director of SYNERGY: UJA-Federation of New York and Synagogues Together at UJA-Federation of New York in New York. She was director of the UAHC-CCAR Commission on Reform Jewish Outreach and the UAHC-CCAR Commission on Synagogue Affiliation from 1991–2005.

since the original team—Moses, Aaron, and Miriam with help from Jethro and a last minute save by Nahshon—set out. On the other hand, they are questions that we urgently address in the context of our own moment. Each writer (and you may notice some interesting characteristics in common here and there with the Exodus team) shares his or her wisdom gained from experience from various vantage points on the way through the contemporary *midbar*. In addition to these considerable gifts, each also shines a light on his or her own passion for a Jewish life of meaning and purpose, reminding us that, although the focus here is on transformation of synagogues, the impact reaches far beyond, certainly to the larger institutions of the Jewish community and into the world, but also deeply into individual lives.

* * *

Jonathan Sarna, in his masterful *American Judaism*, speaks of the late twentieth-century "reawakening of American Jewish life" and "revitalization of Jewish tradition," characterized by interest in spirituality and ritual practice that changed the synagogue, Jewish education, and Jewish culture across all movements. "By the year 2000, the look and feel of American Judaism had changed and many aspects of Jewish religious life were revitalized and transformed."[1] This change was accompanied by a sense of urgency, as well as opportunity, especially toward the turn of the millennium, when "transformation" fever was running high in America. Case in point: the special expanded September 1999 issue of *Sh'ma* led off with the question: "How will we transform synagogues, the central address for much of Jewish life, to reflect the changes and challenges of an emerging Jewish spiritual community?"[2] Sarna further cites the rising rate of intermarriage and anxiety about continuity, as well as the emergence of feminism and spirituality in America, as key drivers of change and concludes, "The only certainty as calls for renewal escalated and the twentieth century receded was that Jewish religious life remained vibrant enough to change."[3]

In 2009 it is still too soon to tell what the ultimate outcome of transformation efforts born in the "awakening" that Sarna identifies will be. However, as the articles that follow attest, even as experiments in new models continue to extend boundaries and develop authentic and meaningful ways to engage an increasingly diverse Jewish population, we are also beginning to assess, consolidate, and even institutionalize what has been learned in the heady pioneering era with an eye to spreading and deepening the impact. This issue of the *CCAR Journal* gives a snapshot of synagogue transformation in the present moment. Its scope is narrow in the sense that it draws almost exclusively from synagogue leaders, scholars, practitioners of the emerging field of synagogue renewal, and institutional leaders connected to the Reform Movement through their training and/or the venue of their work. (Driven by the same demographic and cultural trends, all religious movements as well as independent entrepreneurs are experimenting with new modes of Jewish community-building, all in the context of contemporary American life.) At the same time, its scope is broad in the range of approaches and institutions reflected.

The first section, "Synagogue Transformation: To What End and How?" brings an assessment of where we stand. Isa Aron, founder of the Experiment in Congregational Education (ECE), Lawrence Hoffman, with Ron Wolfson, founder of Synagogue 2000 (S2K, now S3K), have joined colleagues Steven M. Cohen and Ari Y. Kelman in a study of the long-term impact of synagogue change initiatives, which will result in a book to be published later this year. (The study was funded largely by the Cummings Foundation and UJA-Federation of New York, both funders as well of ECE and S2K projects, a fact that is noteworthy as evidence of the broader context in which larger transformation initiatives exist.) They share here two articles based on their research. In "Functional and Visionary Congregations" Steven Cohen and his colleagues begin the discussion by teasing out parameters that describe the ideal transformed congregation, defined as visionary as opposed to functional. Lawrence Hoffman follows with observations from the study on leading change, "Transforming Congregations: What Is Needed, How It Happens, When It Works."

The second section, "Transformation in Action," includes six examples of intentional change or congregational formation. The first two articles describe some of the experiences of two synagogues included in the Aron/Cohen/Hoffman/Kelman study. Both are large, well-resourced flagship congregations that can be seen as intent to move, to borrow Jim Collins' terminology, from "good to great." In "Keeping the Mice in Shul: Principles for Synagogue Transformation," Richard Jacobs distills lessons learned at Westchester Reform Temple through multiple, on-going, integrated efforts to deepen meaningful Jewish engagement for all members. Jeremy Morrison describes one key aspect of Temple

Israel of Boston's sustained pursuit of Isaiah's vision of extending the tent in "The Riverway Project: Engaging Adults in Their 20s and 30s in the Process of Transforming the Synagogue." While maintaining a sense of urgency and embedding a culture of innovation may be particular challenges for these first two congregations, it's a different matter to transform a congregation that is stressed either from demographic loss and/or internal conflict. In "Temple Emanuel of Beverly Hills: A Work in Progress," Laura Geller, who started her rabbinate at Hillel, reflects on the chances both she and the congregation have taken over time to make the changes that have brought them so far. Mitch Chefitz, author and *havurah* guru, and Temple Israel of Miami undertook a different kind of experiment, whose story he tells in "Restoring a Center City Congregation." It's interesting to note that both of these synagogues chose rabbis who came to them with significant alternative, non-synagogue experience and a positive orientation to challenge. Is that a necessary ingredient for success when congregations are severely stressed? Perhaps the most challenging examples, standing as they do outside movement structures, are two congregations developed afresh with great intentionality and purpose in particular, diverse contexts. Lydia Kukoff, long involved in Jewish education, identity formation, and strategic interventions through her leadership of Reform outreach and her work with the Avi Chai Foundation, describes in "A Do-It-Yourself Shul" the founding and growth of the Chatham Synagogue Netivot Torah, which she served as president. Finally, Darren Levine, whose position is defined as executive director rather than rabbi, writes in "Jewish Community Project" about the experience of working with a dynamic, diverse group of young urban pioneers to develop a multi-faceted, meaningful Jewish presence in lower Manhattan in the aftermath of 9/11. Each of these leaders and congregations is unique; each has much to teach about the creative vision, courage, and persistence that are common to all who set out on the path toward transformation.

As stated at the outset, transformation on one level, in this case the synagogue and those it serves, must inevitably be reflected on multiple systemic levels to be successful. The third section, "Sustaining Synagogue Transformation," takes a look at some of the structures that support and inspire synagogues in their efforts. Hebrew Union College-Jewish Institute of Religion has both been affected by the profound changes in the American Jewish context and acted to make changes in the education of Reform clergy, educators, and communal leaders for transformative religious leadership. Aaron Panken distills the highlights in "HUC-JIR and the Creation of Visionary Jewish Leadership." Beyond the central arms of the movement itself and emanating from the deep concern for the future vitality of the American Jewish community on the part of federations, individual philanthropists, and foundations, a number of independent or loosely linked organizations devoted to synagogue transformation have emerged, many of them with their origins in the Reform Movement, but bringing wide experience in diverse fields and new perspectives to their work. "Agents of Change in an Emerging Field: A Conversation" brings together five leaders, some second generation in their organization and some only in their first years of developing their institutions, to discuss their perspectives and their practice as they work with congregations to effect change. Each is a pioneer in a new and still developing field of practice. A number of local federations across the country, spurred by the rising intermarriage rate and committed to the continuity of a vital American Jewish community, have made profound changes in their relationships with synagogues, seeing them not only as venues for fund-raising as they were in the past, but as key institutions to develop and sustain Jewish identity. Boston, Hartford, Los Angeles, New York, Northern New Jersey, Philadelphia, San Diego, San Francisco—these are some of the federated communities that have initiated, in a variety of ways, efforts to strengthen the ability of synagogues to fulfill their potential. Strong local entities devoted to ongoing provision of services, such as strategic planning, leadership and professional development, outreach, and change management, are a new, vital element that supplements movement services, mediates national programs, and enables learning and mentoring across movements in synagogues in proximity to one another. Deborah Joselow, in "Making Change in the *Kehillah*," describes the evolving and broad-based efforts of UJA-Federation of New York, in particular of the Commission on Jewish Identity and Renewal. Philip Warmflash writes of his particular experience in "A Philadelphia Story: Partnership for Change."

Finally, in "Looking Ahead," Amy Sales, a preeminent scholar of synagogue life and change, considers some of the challenges and opportunities that lie over the horizon for synagogues in "Future of the Synagogue."

Acknowledgments

I am tremendously honored to have been invited to guest-edit this volume of the *CCAR Journal* focused on synagogue transformation. My gratitude extends in many directions:

To my teachers and early mentors, Bernard Mehlman, Ronne Friedman, and Lydia Kukoff, without whom I would not have found my work;

To all the writers, many of whom I have worked alongside at the URJ, HUC-JIR or UJA-Federation of New York, some of whom I have been privileged to teach, and all of whom have taught me;

To Isa Aron, Aron Hirt-Manheimer, Lawrence Hoffman, Deborah Joselow, Alisa Rubin Kurshan, Robert Leventhal, Hayim Herring, Riv-Ellen Prell, Amy Sales, Rob Weinberg and my *hevrah* of federation-based synagogue renewal professionals—Judy Beck, Marv Goodman, David Trietsch and Phil Warmflash for their help and suggestions in framing the issue;

To congregational leaders in the hundreds of congregations with which I have worked, most of whom shy away from speaking of their role in transforming their synagogues, but who nevertheless carry out their responsibilities day after day with steadfastness and love;

Most especially, to Jon Stein for his curiosity, his friendship, and his trust.

Dru Greenwood
October 27, 2009

Postscript

What was in its conception envisioned as an interim snapshot of synagogue transformation efforts—perhaps a check-in part way through the *midbar*—has in the course of the past few weeks taken on a different valence. Most of the articles in this volume were written during the late spring and summer of 2008, the time during our Torah reading cycle when we read Deuteronomy and rehearse the experience and seek to embed the learning from the redemption and revelation we shared on the way from Egypt to the land of promise. In retrospect, how apt! As the issue goes to press, the dislocations resulting from the economic turmoil of the Fall of 2008 are beginning to reverberate throughout all sectors of American society, reaching into synagogue life as well. There is a general feeling of being poised over a precipice, a place where change will not require creating a sense of urgency, but will be driven instead by immanent necessity, a sensibility much more closely aligned with the tenor of the Genesis stories we are in the midst of reading. It appears that, within this changed context, a new era of synagogue change is upon us as well. All the more so, may the hard-won wisdom articulated with such passion in these pages provide good ground for meeting the challenges and the changes ahead. (DG, December 3, 2008)

Notes

1. Jonathan Sarna, *American Judaism* (New Haven: Yale University Press, 2004), pp. 323–324.
2. *Sh'ma*, vol. 30, no. 564, p. 1.
3. Sarna, op. cit., p. 355.

Functional and Visionary Congregations[1]

Isa Aron, Steven M. Cohen, Lawrence Hoffman, and Ari Y. Kelman[2]

With about 80 percent of American Jews belonging to synagogues at some point in their lives, few would doubt that the synagogue is a critical gateway to deepening the Jewish commitments of its members. But not all synagogues are equally adept in maximizing this potential. In too many the gateway functions more like a turn-stile, having little or no impact on those who stream through. One rabbi calls this phenomenon the "façade of success":

> Every Saturday morning there are 50 cars or 100 cars parked in the parking lot. But, every Saturday morning it's a different 50 or 100 cars, depending on that week's bar mitzvah. The sanctuary is full, but no one is becoming very Jewish.

On the other hand, we all know of congregations that regularly transform many previously indifferent members into committed and practicing Jews. What enables these congregations to leave an indelible impression on the lives of congregants and build truly meaningful Jewish communities? In this article, and in a forthcoming book, we argue that these life-changing congregations, which we call "visionary," share a constellation of characteristics that distinguish them from a much larger group of congregations, which we call "functional."

For the past three years we have been engaged in a study of some extraordinary synagogues, observing at each congregation, and

ISA ARON is Professor of Jewish Education, Rhea Hirsch School of Education, HUC-JIR Los Angeles, California.

STEVEN M. COHEN is Research Professor of Jewish Social Policy, HUC-JIR New York, New York.

LAWRENCE HOFFMAN (NY69 and Ph.D. C73) is Professor of Liturgy, HUC-JIR New York, New York.

ARI Y. KELMAN is Associate Professor of History, University of California, Davis, California.

conducting close to 150 interviews. The eight synagogues we chose to study in depth all underwent one or more intentional change processes in the past two decades, either on their own or as part of a national project, like Synagogue 2000 (S2K) or the Experiment in Congregational Education (ECE). They vary in size, region, surrounding population density, Jewish population size, leadership style, and resources; three are affiliated with the Conservative Movement and five with the Reform Movement. These variations notwithstanding, we found that the leaders of these eight synagogues share an essential feature: vivid and coherent visions of the congregation they seek to become.

Reflecting on the images of success that leaders of these congregations carry with them, we posit two contrasting "ideal types," clusters of characteristics at opposite ends of a continuum. One composite, for which we have chosen the term "visionary," represents a congregation that has articulated and enacted a powerful and widely shared vision of a sacred community. In contrast, the congregation we call "functional" provides a set of discrete functions and services for its consumer-oriented members.

Since "visionary" and "functional" are theoretical constructs, none of the synagogues in our study fully meets all the criteria of "visionary." Similarly, there are probably very few congregations that are altogether "functional." Nonetheless, these constructs have more than academic interest. They point to the essential difference between mediocrity and excellence in contemporary synagogues in North America, one embodied in the distinctions between truly visionary congregations and those that are merely functional.

The Functional Congregation

Functional congregations certainly work, and may even function quite well, in providing professionally delivered high-quality services of all kinds. They generally appeal to their congregants as fitting venues for the celebration of a bar or bat mitzvah, for worship services on the High Holidays, and for the availability of the rabbi to attend to weddings, funerals, and hospital visits. But the functional congregation lacks a compelling, widely shared, and deep-seated vision that would make it truly great. The key ingredients of the functional congregation include: a consumerist orientation, segmentation, passivity, detachment, lack of reflectiveness, and routinization. Each bears elaboration.

Consumerist Purpose

In functional congregations, a culture of **consumerism** characterizes the relationship between dues-paying congregant and service-providing congregation. In order to attend High Holiday services, congregants pay annual dues. To celebrate the bar/bat mitzvah of a child, to take another example, the children attend religious school for a certain number of years. Reform leaders estimate that approximately half of congregants in the Reform Movement leave the congregation after the bar or bat mitzvah of the youngest child. (The comparable rates are substantially lower for families in Conservative congregations, and lower still for Orthodox households.) During the period of membership little is demanded and little is invested; and by the end of the relationship, little of sustained Judaic value is achieved.

Segmented Functioning

Along with a consumerist approach comes a highly rationalized and **segmented** approach to the congregation's structure and functioning. In such a setting, services are produced and delivered discretely, in segments, with little relationship to one another. The domains of worship, the religious school, hospital visitation, adult programming, social action, and administration all function independently, rather than in concert.

Segmentation is manifest in several domains. The architecture of many congregations creates a physical separation between the sanctuary, classrooms, and meeting rooms. This separation is mirrored by a strict division of labor, with the clergy attending to worship, the educator to study, and so on. Board meetings are taken up with administrative matters, with little attention to personal meaning and engagement, and little reference to overall purpose.

While individual programs and activities may engage congregants, the lack of synergy between them reinforces the consumerist orientation. As one former congregation president notes:

> The congregation [of the past] is well intended. Everyone wants to make the Hebrew school better, do more outreach, be more responsive to new members, have more of a warm, fuzzy feeling about themselves. Everybody wants that, and you can set up a committee to try to implement it. You have all these ideas, but does it have follow through? Does it become the culture? Is the congregation

imbued with that attitude? Does it become holistic or just individual activities?

Passivity

In functional congregations' highly rationalized service-delivery systems, trained and expert professionals—clergy, educators, and administrators—produce, manage, market, and deliver the sought-after services. The excessive reliance on highly skilled professionals comes with a price: **passivity**, a condition marked by congregants' lack of active participation and lack of psychic engagement in congregational activity.

The mitzvah of *bikur holim* becomes the near-exclusive province of the clergy. Parents drop off their children at religious school, handing over full educational responsibility to professional school directors. The board leaves real decision-making to the rabbi, other professionals, and a small, inner circle of donors and volunteers.

Passivity has both quantitative and qualitative dimensions. Quantitatively, it connotes low rates of attendance and participation at congregational events, programs, and activities. Qualitatively, it implies little genuine enthusiasm for, or engagement in, the events, even among those who bother to show.

Detachment

Closely related to passivity is the detachment experienced in worship, learning, and other congregational activities. Functional communities fail to excite, provoke, mobilize, inspire, or provide substantial significance to worshippers, learners, and congregants. The common experience in such congregations may be pleasant, familial, and familiar, but lacks transcendence, engagement, and sacredness.

Congregants who participate in activities that carry little in the way of real significance, purpose, or meaning may do so out of a sense of obligation to a decreasingly compelling tradition. They may attend by dint of sheer intra-familial compulsion. ("I go because my spouse wants me to go." "I go to set a good example for my children.") But these congregants are detached; they fail to bring intentionality or derive much real meaning from these activities. Reflecting on why she was so keen on changing services at her congregation, one woman recalls:

I began to think about the fact that, yes, the services were routine and the words didn't have any meaning particularly. You went because you wanted to be there and because it was a connection and a community, but the services were really not grabbing in any particular way.

Resistance to Change

Leaders in functional congregations tend to be slow to respond to changing cultural and demographic patterns. Wedded to conventions that have worked in the past, they believe that change is unnecessary; even if admitting it might be beneficial, they find it difficult and unsettling.

The commitment of synagogue leaders to the routine, and **their resistance to change**—the fifth major characteristic of the "functional congregation"—may stem from attachment to tradition or from fear of the unknown. Long-standing leaders are skilled in the old ways, wary of leaving their comfort zone, and find it awkward to learn new approaches.

Unreflective Leadership

Resistance to change is due, in part, perhaps in large part, to **a low level of reflection,** the sixth and final feature of the "functional" congregation. Synagogues, like other organizations, can perceive, learn, reflect, internalize, and adapt— or not. When they do so, they effectively learn from their changing environments; they critically assess their performance; they develop and ingrain new insights and patterns of action; and they come to adaptively change their dysfunctional behavior. All too often, however, their leaders are too busy or too defensive to think critically and imaginatively about abiding customs and habits.

Summarizing the Functional Congregation

The foregoing description of the functional congregation may be summarized as follows:

1. Consumerist purpose: the fee-for-service arrangements provide consumers with discrete services, in particular, education of children for ceremonial celebration of bar/bat mitzvah and clergy officiation at life-cycle ceremonies.

2. Segmented understanding: parts, relationships, programs stand on their own, with little integration of worship, learning, caring, social engagement, or community.

3. Passivity and excessive professional control: worshippers sit passively, parents drop off children for religious schooling, caring is left to the clergy.

4. Detachment, rote performance of scripted interactions, with little genuine significance or feelings of transcendent connection to Jews and Judaism.

5. Resistance to change prevents serious consideration of alternative modes and structures.

6. Unreflective leadership focuses on established practices, programs, and institutional arrangements rather than on purpose and vision.

The "Visionary Congregation"

Six key features characterize "functional" congregations; an equal number of contrasting features characterize the opposite ideal type, the "visionary" congregation. These desirable qualities are: sacred purpose, holistic ethos, participatory culture, meaningful engagement, innovative disposition, and reflective leadership.

Sacred Purpose, Sacred Community

At the heart of the "visionary" congregation is an overarching commitment to **sacred purpose**, a commitment that suffuses all aspects of its functioning. Where the functional congregation delivers specified services to consumer-clients, its visionary counterparts provides sacred experiences to engaged members of a holy community (recall the traditional Hebrew terminology for synagogues, *Kehillah Kedoshah*).

References to sacred community or the sense of a sacred purpose emerged repeatedly in our interviews. David Rokoff, a past lay leader at Temple Beth Elohim of Wellesley, Mass., remarked:

> Synagogue 2000 exposed us to a methodology of creating sacred community based on knowledge and experimentation with new things. It gave us a different way of looking at what "authentic" meant.

As befitting the notion of sacredness, the holy work of the congregation is intimately connected to God. Josh Seidman, a mid-thirties congregant at Temple Micah in Washington D.C., found sacred meaning in "Micah House," a congregationally sponsored transitional shelter for homeless woman:

> [H]owever we conceive of God, ... this [Micah House] is God's work. ... So, I bring that spiritual mindset to my board meeting. We started off beginning every session with some sort of prayer, or poem, or song.

When sacred purpose comes to be thoroughly infused throughout the culture of the congregation, it can offer members a powerful sense of obligation and mutual responsibility. "People are more committed to an organization when they have meaningful work to do, when they feel a sense of attachment to others in the group, and when they see the group as representing a moral good that allows them to transcend merely personal interest."[3] In our terms, communities that produce what we may call "sacred product" are more able to elicit loyalty and generate commitment among its members, both to the community and to each other. Peter Wang, an active lay leader at Westchester Reform Temple remarks:

> [O]ne of the things we talk a lot about now is the sense of covenant, the idea that people should understand that being a member has obligations as well as benefits. With that we still have a ways to go. I think there is still a sense, certainly in the community in which we live, of entitlement. What are you going to do for me as opposed to what am I expected to do for you? So, I think we still have some way to go to have people understand their sense of responsibility and the obligation that comes with being a member of the synagogue.

Holistic Ethos

Visionary communities maintain a holistic ethos, one that sees the parts as integrally related to the whole and attempts to minimize boundaries between people, programs, institutions, groups, and space. It rejects dualisms such as particularism vs. universalism, education vs. entertainment, study vs. action. It attempts to transcend the segmentation of functions common in ordinary congregations and the atomistic view of the congregation as apart from everyday life, the neighborhood, the Jewish community, the larger society, or the world.

In communities operating in a holistic fashion, worship services, involvement with one's child's religious education, caring for others, adult education, and social justice initiatives all serve as portals of entry into increased congregational engagement. When applied to prayer and worship, holistic thinking inspires such elements as text teaching as part of the service, creating a welcoming atmosphere, prayers for healing, and even recognizing the value of providing good food at the end of services. In the area of education, it holds that learning is as a life-long process. Jewish learning can (and should) occur everywhere, not only in a classroom. More broadly, a consciousness of Jewish learning permeates all arenas of synagogue activity. Margie Miller, a lay leader in Westchester Reform Temple, comments:

> Before ECE, religious school, the early childhood program, committee meetings and services for congregants, etc. were separate. Now they are more connected. ECE became the glue that held them together.

A holistic approach also serves to diminish many of the more common social boundaries separating the congregational community from the larger population. Of particular concern are those congregants who see themselves, or have been seen by others, as marginal to Judaism in general or to the particular congregation. Visionary congregations minimize instances in which congregants feel excluded, unwelcome, or uncomfortable.

Participatory Culture, Participating Congregants

Judaism and Jewish culture are highly participatory. Jews are expected to play active and engaged roles in ritual, culture, and community. The *mitzvot* obligate everyone, not just the clergy. Consistent with the participatory ethos of Judaism, visionary congregations abide and nurture a culture of participation.

This issue can be explored through the lens of the shifting approaches to Jewish prayer over time. The traditional prayer service is marked by chanting and singing out loud in approximate unison, and by individual prayer that comes together at intervals. In the transition to modernity, particularly in the nineteenth century, several factors militated against broad participation by worshippers. Westernized and modernized Jews came to see the traditional style of communal prayer as disorganized, indecorous, and contrary to the Western spiritual aesthetic they had internalized. Reform temples in Germany and the United States, in particular, but synagogues in the other denominations as well, adopted a worship style that was more scripted, organized, decorous, and seemingly more reverential. Congregants expected rabbis and cantors to maintain an aura of aloofness and hierarchical distance from the laity. Abraham Joshua Heschel's words, first written in the 1940s, still ring true today, albeit perhaps not as ubiquitously as in his time:

> We have developed the habit of praying by proxy. Many congregants seem to have adopted the principle of vicarious prayer. ..... Men and women would not raise their voices, unless the rabbi issues the signal. Alas, they have come to regard the rabbi as a master of ceremonies.[4]

This aloof and hierarchical relationship was given physical expression in the standard spatial arrangements of most congregations' sanctuaries. There, rabbis and cantors performed on raised platforms in front of well-dressed "audiences" of orderly and respectful worshippers seated in the pews.

The Havurah movement of the 1970s challenged an ethos of congregational life that they saw as passive, disempowering, hierarchical, and inauthentic. In contradistinction, they constructed worship services of small, intimate communities, where worshippers sat in the round and often on the floor, and where liturgical leadership rested upon the laity who eschewed the notion of being "led" formally. The very title of the movement's best-known and most widely read publication, *The Jewish Catalog; A Do-It-Yourself Kit*, speaks to the goal of "liberating" lay Jews from dependence on rabbis and other professional Jews in line with the participatory spirit of the times.

In recent years, the urge for greater participation in worship services has provoked controversy and changes around music and the role of the cantor. Reform congregations, with their liturgical flexibility and the availability of musical instruments, have moved to make worship services more musically accessible and engaging. And this participatory culture extends beyond the worship service to embrace learning, caring for the community, and social justice. Educational directors at the visionary congregations make parental engagement in their children's education a key objective. Visiting the sick and comforting the bereaved, to take just two examples of the caring community, are a shared responsibility, rather than being relegated to the clergy. Everyone, not just the staff, is obligated to work for social justice, not just on mitzvah day, but in an ongoing fashion. Joel Sisenwine, rabbi of Temple Beth Elohim, argues that participation is key in synagogue governance as well:

> [Y]ou have to allow [lay leaders] a place to fail and to succeed. It is necessary for them to grow Jewishly. There's a tendency for synagogues to hire professionals to ensure that they don't fail, but that is the death knell of a strong community.

Meaningful Engagement

A major theme in the study of American religion over the last two decades has been the rise in the phenomenon of meaning-seeking on the part of Americans of all faiths. With the decline in the power of received doctrine, the pluralization of meaning-systems, the expansion of the freedom of individual choice, and the loosening of institutional ties, Americans have increasingly engaged in a search for meaning, be it in their religious communities or elsewhere.[5] As a result, authority moves from received traditions and their interpreters (clergy, parents, educators) to the realm of individual experience and individuals' search for meaning.

Charles Liebman was, in the 1980s, among the first to explicitly note the shift among Jews. Drawing upon the earlier work of Marshall Sklare,[6] he called attention to a growing attitude of "personalism," "the tendency to transform and evaluate the [Jewish] tradition in terms of its utility of significance to the individual."[7] He contrasted the new personalism with the classic Jewish traditional approach to religious obligation: "Personal choice is endowed with spiritual sanctity, and contrary to past tradition it is always considered more virtuous than performing an act out of a sense of obedience to God." A search for personal meaning and personalized religious experience has come to characterize much of American Jews in the last third of the twentieth century.[8] Current and potential congregants choose to affiliate and to become more or less involved in congregational life based, in part, upon the extent to which such involvement provides them with genuine and rewarding meaning.

Visionary congregations, then, are intent and purposeful (and successful) about the delivery of Jewish meaning to their congregants. Their leaders think explicitly and carefully about such matters and are willing to innovate to continue to deliver meaningful experiences to their ever-changing congregants.

As noted earlier, the issue of liturgical music and how to use it to best effect to make services meaningful is of ongoing concern to cantors and rabbis alike. For Teddy Klaus, Music Director of Temple Micah, the ultimate test of the music he prepares, oversees, and performs in prayer services does not lie strictly within the realm of aesthetic quality. Rather, he judges the success of the music for which he is responsible in terms of its spiritual impact upon the worshippers, its ability to convey and deliver spiritual meaning:

> What I do at the Temple is not just about music. It is actually deeper than that. If we are trying musically to compete with Lincoln Center, we're going to fail....What we were working towards within worship was deeper. It was about bringing prayer to people and liturgy to life. It's not just about the music. I really believe that what some people call a "dumbed down melody" is only as bad or good, to put it positively, as the *kavanah* of the person presenting it.

Innovative Disposition

Susan Wolfe, board member of Congregation Beth Am in Los Altos Hills, California, remarks:

> When you attempt change you have to be willing to fail. It doesn't all work. At Beth Am we've had failures—big failures. Then we step back and regroup and revamp and then try to do it better the next time. But if you don't make any mistakes, you don't learn anything.

Ric Rudman, a former president at Beth Am, concurs:

> Every ten years or so you should take all the things you really cherish and zero base them. What do we know now? What's the current reality? Where do you want to be in five years? And what changes do we have to make in the current model to get there? That will lead to some new things and improvements in the system.

Change and innovation have been at the heart of conflicts and controversies within Jewish communities since their inception. In the American context, proponents of innovation have generally argued that failure to change will leave Judaism incapable of attracting a more sophisticated, acculturated, integrated, and modernized younger generation. Opponents of change argue that proposed changes contradict time-honored values of Judaism. In their view, minor adjustments, rather than wholesale ransacking of established and well-functioning patterns, can succeed in bridging the apparent gaps between the ways of the past and the tastes of the future.

Synagogue leaders differ about the pace and direction of change. In general, Conservative congregations introduced changes very slowly, often mindful of the comfort level of their older congregants. Among the Reform congregations in our study, Temple Beth Elohim pursued change most aggressively, bringing in an entirely new professional staff with an explicit mandate for change. It is, as educator Alison Kur, notes, "an entrepreneurial congregation. They enjoy experimentation." Joel Sisenwine recalls his first two year:

> I bombarded them with change. We were standing for *shema* one week and sitting the next. The only thing you knew when you entered the door was that you were going to experience change. We spent hours on worship. Every week, we would focus on how to change things. We were very disciplined in that way. How much to move the community and how much to settle in. Within a year, not one thing about the service was the same.

Reflective Leadership

For years social scientists have been tracking the ever-quickening pace of change in technology, culture, and society. The rapidity and unevenness of change, some say, generate greater diversity within populations and markets, and more rapid cultural shifts over time and over generational cohorts. Whatever the true extent, scope, and magnitude of diversity and change, management experts have been nearly unanimous in proclaiming that corporations and the people who lead them need to develop the tools to make sense of the changing world around them, to perceive both emerging obstacles and emerging opportunities, to manage adaptation and innovation, to assess their results, and to adjust one's actions in light of one's assessment and ever-changing circumstances.

Innovation just doesn't happen on its own. It demands ongoing reflection and attention, as well as a readiness to deliberate and learn, as Rabbi Rick Jacobs of Westchester Reform Temple makes clear:

> ECE gave us the tools we used in our transformation work. We came to believe strongly that learning informs change, whatever change we want. If we want to change our Tikkun Olam program, if we want to change worship, we don't just ask the rabbis and the cantors to make the changes. Instead we gathered a wide cross-section of lay people and professionals to learn, think, experiment, and refine.

A reflective disposition requires constant attention and rein-forcement. Reflective leadership and decision-making, then, embrace the conceptual thinking, critical examination of current practice, exploration of successful alternative, and deliberative application of lessons learned to one's own situation.

Daryl Messinger, former president and volunteer coordinator of the Shabbaton program at Beth Am, emphasizes the synagogue's commitment to the ongoing feedback, learning, adaptation, and feedback again— marks of a true learning organization, committed to ongoing reflection:

> All along we said Shabbaton is an experiment. But it became very clear that in year 5 or 6 that people stopped believing this. So we needed to say "OK, [loudly] IT IS AN EXPERIMENT. It's going to keep changing. We need your input, this is why we're evaluating." We then became much more explicit in the last two years about the changes made each year, and that that came from last year's feed-back. So people wanted more retreats and less structure; we did more of those; then people came back and said we want more struc-ture. But that's how you keep it feeling like an experiment, not a cookie cutter.

Rabbi Jonah Pesner, formerly of Temple Israel of Boston, points to how reflectiveness, even in a functional congregation, requires constant attention and reinforcement. Congregations can strive for transformation and excellence. They can even embed the elements of excellence deep into their organizational cultures. They can profit repeatedly from excellent performance. But retaining a reflective stance toward something as seemingly mundane as the congregational calendar requires a constant awareness and ability to recall and apply the principles of a visionary congregation:

> [T]he temptation at our calendar meeting is, "Well, these are the programs we do, let's put them up on the calendar." And again and again the people on the staff keep agitating us ourselves on, "Why are we putting that on the calendar? Just because we've always done it? Shouldn't we consider where people are?" What we kept coming to was: Let's get together a group of lay leaders and have them talk to us about what should adult learning on Israel look like. Let's see what they want to own. What do they want to create out of that?

The Visionary Congregation: Summing Up

We summarize our description of the visionary congregation as follows:

1. **Sacred purpose** is a pervasive, shared vision that infuses all aspects of the synagogue.
2. **Holistic ethos**: the parts are related to each other and to the whole; ritual, learning, caring, social engagement, and community appear in several areas of functioning; lay and professional leadership function cooperatively; boundaries within and around the community are more porous and fluid.
3. **Participatory** culture, on all levels: congregants, students, lay leaders, professionals, and parents engage in the work of the sacred community.
4. **Meaningful engagement**, achieved through repeated inspirational experiences that provide genuine meaning to people's lives.
5. **Innovation disposition**, marked by a search for diversity and alternatives, a tolerance of failure, ability to address and overcome resistance to change, and a willingness to abandon less functional ways of doing things.
6. **Reflective leadership** and governance, marked by careful examination of alternatives, a commitment to overarching purpose, attention to relationships, mastery of detail, and a planful approach to change.

Given the nature of American Jewry and the exigencies of contemporary life, it is unlikely that any synagogue will ever be perfectly "visionary." But surveying the landscape of congregational life, we see many attempts to choose sacredness over consumerism, holism over segmentation, participation over passivity, engagement over detachment, innovation over convention, and reflection over mindless routines.

The journey from functional to visionary is long and arduous. Along the path are any number of recalcitrant players: congregants who have no interest in joining a sacred community; professionals who fear letting go of the routines they have developed over the years; congregants unable to acknowledge that worship styles that are meaningful to them are not working for the next generation; leaders who have a hard time letting go of power. But there are also professionals who discover a new meaning to their work; congregants who feel fulfilled applying their expertise to creating a stronger synagogue; congregants who are amazed to find within themselves a talent for leadership; and, most importantly, congregants who discover that they thrive on text study, or worship, or creating a caring community, or working for social justice, or (best of all) a combination of all of these.

In our forthcoming book, *Sacred Strategies: Transforming Functional Synagogues into Visionary Congregations*, we examine the journey from "function" to "vision" in our eight congregations, as it played out in the arenas of *torah, avodah*, and *gemilut hasadim*. We narrate in depth the contours of the journey and place that journey in the context of organizational theory. We hope that our research will contribute to a spirited discussion about the types of synagogues we need and what it takes to become such a synagogue.

Notes

1. Adapted from I. Aron, S.M. Cohen, L. Hoffman, and A.Y. Kelman, *Sacred Strategies: Transforming Functional Synagogues into Visionary Congregations* (Woodstock, Vt.: Jewish Lights Publishing, forthcoming, 2009).

2. The authors would like to thank the following federations, foundation, and individuals for their generous support of our research: the Commission on Jewish Identity and Renewal of UJA-Federation of New York; The Nathan Cummings Foundation; The Combined Jewish Philanthropies of Boston; Synagogue 3000; Mr. Arthur Winn; and The Esther F. and William J. Bushman Beth Shalom Endowment Fund of the Jewish Community Foundation of Greater Kansas City.

3. N.T. Ammerman and A.E. Farnsley, *Congregation & Community* (New

Brunswick, N.J.: Rutgers University Press, 1997), p. 51.

4. A.J. Heschel, *Man's Quest for God* (Santa Fe, N.M.: Aurora Press, 1954/ 1996), p. 50.

5. For example, see: R.N. Bellah et al., *Habits of the Heart: Individualism and Commitment in American Life* (Berkeley, Calif.: University of California Press, 1985); R. Wuthnow, *Loose Connections: Joining Together in America's Fragmented Communities* (Cambridge, Mass.: Harvard University Press, 1998); W.C. Roof, *Spiritual Marketplace: Baby Boomers and the Remaking of American Religion* (Princeton, N.J.: Princeton University Press, 1999); A. Wolfe, *The Transformation of American Religion: How We Actually Live Our Faith* (New York: Simon and Schuster, 2003); S.M. Cohen and A.M. Eisen, *The Jew Within: Self, Family, and Community in America* (Bloomington, Ind.: Indiana University Press, 2000).

6. M. Sklare, *Jewish Identity on the Suburban Frontier: A Study of Group Survival in the Open Society* (Chicago, Ill.: University of Chicago Press, 1979).

7. C.S. Liebman and S.M. Cohen, *Two Worlds of Judaism: The Israeli and American Experiences* (New Haven, Ct.: Yale University Press, 1992), p. 128.

8. See, for example, R.E. Prell, *Prayer & Community: The Havurah in American Judaism* (Detroit, Mich.: Wayne State University Press, 1989); S.M. Cohen and A. M. Eisen, *The Jew Within: Self, Family, and Community in America* (Bloomington, Ind.: Indiana University Press, 2000); and B. Horowitz, *Connections and Journeys: Assessing Critical Opportunities for Enhancing Jewish Identity* (New York: UJA-Federation of New York, 2003).

Transforming Congregations: What It Needs, How It Happens, When It Works[1]

Lawrence Hoffman

Asking what constitutes a transformed congregation is like inquiring after the definition of a good novel. One kind of answer is *substantive*, identification in terms of *content*: I like *War and Peace*; you like *Moby Dick*. Substantive definitions are arbitrary. So too with synagogue transformation. My colleagues (Isa Aron, Steven Cohen and Ari Kelman) and I want transformation according to the criteria we call "visionary"; others think transformation should do something else. Substantive identifications of transformation too are a matter of taste.

Another kind of answer is *formal*. Both *War and Peace* and *Moby Dick* are great novels because they obey formal criteria—they must prove lasting, let us say, or have memorable characters and a consuming plot.

This article handles the *formal* characteristics of transformed congregations. People may legitimately take issue with our *substantive* preference for "visionary," without, however, questioning the *formal* qualities that would define "transformation." The issue here is how synagogues transform themselves, regardless of what transformative end they choose.

Formally speaking, then, a synagogue counts as trans*form*ed, if:

1. It *thinks differently.*
2. Its change is *pervasive*, showing up, eventually, even in its board, its offices, its literature, its organization of space, its "everything."

LAWRENCE HOFFMAN (NY69 and Ph.D. C73) is Professor of Liturgy, HUC-JIR New York, New York.

3. Its *change proves lasting*, beyond just the first flush of success.

4. It experiences a genuine *alteration in institutional culture*.

After extended interviews with key people in eight synagogues that underwent transformation, we think we can say a good deal now about how synagogues go about fulfilling these criteria.

How Change Started

Even transformed synagogues begin with ordinary people who join synagogues for ordinary reasons: to educate children, meet friends, "get a bar/bat mitzvah," and so on. But for some, something happens: they encounter a turning point in their lives, where they begin looking for "something more." We call these *nodal moments*, points at which people sense the need for new direction. They are ready to find something in synagogues that they never knew was there. "You know when you blow glass and it's hot and you can mold it?" asks Agudath Israel's Paula Mack Drill. "That happens when people are at really critical junctures." For Nancy Belsky at Beth Elohim, herself a psychotherapist, "I was in my own psycho-analysis professionally... so I was open to searching in general." For Terry Rosenberg, "My father was a very big influence on my life .... When my daughter became bat mitzvah, he had died, and I was very moved and melancholy about what all this meant."

Everyone meets up with nodal moments at some time or other. Great synagogues appreciate this human encounter with life's inevitable voids, and offer in return not just programming, but an opportunity to matter. "Mattering" has two aspects. *Internally*, it denotes a sense of wholeness, satisfaction because "I matter." *Externally*, people discover that they do not just matter; they matter *to others*— they make a difference somewhere in the congregation or the larger world beyond.

The rabbis too were sometimes in nodal moments, usually at that stage of their calling when going through the usual motions as busy synagogue clergy had become routine; as trusted senior rabbis, they were in a position to accomplish something significant and lasting.

Change is most likely to begin when laypeople in nodal moments find rabbis of similar temperament, anxious to make a difference and offering opportunities to matter. Together, rabbis and laypeople create a change team.

Team Work

Gadflies with D'n'A

The rabbinic change agents we met directed institutions that by any rational standard are at the top of the synagogue heap. There was no obvious reason to change course. But they were possessed by "D'n'A"—D[iscontent] '[a]n[d]' A[mbition]. They wanted to go beyond what we call the three "B"s—"busy, big, and boisterous." Without a vision, however, their ambition to innovate had nowhere to go.

Developing a Vision

Most rabbis had first to overcome other people's satisfaction with the status quo, often with radical measures to get people's attention. In a sermon entitled, "Ending Religious School as We Know It," Rabbi Rick Jacobs pleaded, "The thing is broken and we're going to fix it. It's not about changing Hebrew school by fifteen minutes or getting a new Hebrew text book. That's small, little, thinking." Rabbi Elaine Zecher says wryly, "People sometimes need to perceive an institutional trauma to make things happen."

But trauma alone just traumatizes; good rabbis convert trauma into vision. This is where intervention programs became important. New visions require new language and interventions provided that language. Eventually, congregations adapted these national visions to their own local needs. But first, they imported new vocabulary offered by the national interventions, "Congregation of learners," for example, and "Sacred Community."

Assembling Teams

As we saw, lay support came from people at life's nodal moments. Because these moments are intensely personal, they required a personal response: a rabbinic letter or phone call (or both) requesting participation. By definition, ideal team members are busy elsewhere. Only personal appeals would get them to add yet one more cause to their agenda of responsibilities.

At this point, a subtle sense of elitism helped things along. Team members were proud of being personally recruited, and felt the added cachet of joining experimental programs offered by people whom they trusted to be on the cutting edge of things. Excitement built as teams came together around the possibility of becoming (in Rick Jacobs' words) "this little heated core of really great bold thinking. People would say, 'ECE is going to be the wave of the future, and our temple….' There was a little bit of being puffed up, I think – 'Oh we're the chosen few.'" Temple Micah's Josh Seidman comments, "There was a little bit of an 'inside the group, outside the group' thing… there was the group that was studying, and then there was the rest of the congregation."

At times, this elitism proved a stumbling block, as teams discovered a gap between their own heightened expectations and everyone else. When Josh returned from his fist S2K conference, he found congregants thinking, "We were from Mars. How do we try to bring back that sort of excitement and spiritual connection without scaring people?" Teams faced the challenge of visioning ahead of the congregation but then slowing down to bring the rest of the congregation along.

Field Work

As if following Hillel's adage to "Go out and see what the people are doing" successful teams visited the most remarkable places. Harold Gillman in Beth Israel remembers, "a church down the street over here… and we went in and said, 'Wow, We like that.'" Congregations that failed to change visited alternatives too, but found reasons why what they saw would not work for them, whereas congregations intent on change found at least something that just might. "Don't adopt; adapt" went an S2K motto. Visionary congregations did; functional congregations did not.

Sustaining Team Momentum

People joined the team because of a personal invitation. But why did they stay? Who were these people?

Most of them were the regulars, the same people who do everything else at the synagogue. But there were also people who would never have gotten involved had they not received that initial phone call. Why did the latter, especially, persist? One reason was the excitement of the conversation. Teams took special pride in the "rush" of mutual discovery. Beth Shalom's Susie Drazen remembers, "We're ping-ponging stuff off each other and sharing information… what can we do better? What really worked? What do we need to be aware of?"

The interventions managed to avoid the usual hassles that boards and committees rehash. ECE set up salon discussions called "community conversations." S2K deepened conversation by restructuring meetings around curricular study and a personal check-in that reinforced commitment to one another. "We felt an instant connection to other families," says team member Bob Miller. "If I saw somebody on a train or in the community, we would have something in common. It was a nice connection."

But more than friendship was at stake. People felt privileged to do something supremely important. Along the way, they grew personally in learning, collegiality, and excitement.

Mutual Discovery

This shared thrill of breaking new ground usually goes by the word "collaboration," but we have to be careful how we use that term, since it is sometimes thought to denote a flat leadership style whereby everything is allowed to bubble up from group process. We distinctly did not find that here. In most cases, change was driven by a single and singular visionary, almost always the rabbi. Our rabbis were "collaborative," however, in the sense of being transparent rather than secretive, and treating lay leaders as dialogue partners. The rabbis benefited in return, in that (says Terry Rosenberg), "We said to the rabbi, 'Look, you can go out and do something really radical in the synagogue and if anybody gives you a hard time, you have the whole Synagogue 2000 initiative behind you.'"

Signs of Success

Shifting Boundaries

With cooperative team work, roles and boundaries became porous. On the clergy level, it was not always clear where the rabbi's work ended and the cantor's began. Beth Elohim's cantor, Jodi Sufrin, for instance, says happily, "I find that I am working harder than ever with a broad range of responsibilities. It's interesting that music does not take up a large percentage of my time." Also, responsibilities that had once been assumed to lie with the professional staff were given to congregants. Celia Shapiro at Temple Micah explains: "It is pretty common now that if a group of people—well, for instance, last year a bunch of people wanted to read Yehudah Amichai. All they have to do is tell the board and the board says OK and they set up a group."

We call this phenomenon *"the decentralization"* of authority. It is not as if the traditional locus of authority, the rabbi, loses anything.

On the contrary, Rabbi/Cantor Angela Buchdahl reflected what we saw wherever we looked, when she observed, "The clergy here are pretty much revered."

Dezoning the Synagogue

Functional synagogues are often plagued by religious zoning, the *de facto* assignment of distinct sectors of synagogue life as personal fiefdoms of the professionals charged with running them: for music, the cantor; for schooling, the educator; and so on. The various programming heads then report to the rabbi (sometimes via an executive director), who functions as CEO. On the lay side, each sector is overseen by a different committee; all committees answer to the executive committee or board, at the top of which stands the chair. This segmented system impedes novel thinking, since the authorities with power to effect change are socially located inside hermetically sealed bubbles of activity. The only people who see it all are the rabbi and president. Ordinary congregants rarely think to initiate ideas, since the bureaucratic journey to the locus of authority is not worth the effort.

Porous boundaries, the breakdown of informal zoning regulations, and the spread of communication across silos are all of a piece: Smoothly functioning congregations obey limitations of zoning, because precisely that zoning makes functioning so easy. Spatially, the school wing runs smoothly, but separately from the sanctuary; the ritual committee need not consult with the education committee; cantor and education director hardly ever meet.

But life is holistic. Religious school students sometimes want to pray; *minyan* members enjoy studying. Stretch that example, and you get a synagogue ski trip to the Rockies, where the skiers also pray and study. Under the old system, that falls into no one's zone of authority, so it doesn't happen; and the ski slopes, which are geographically outside the synagogue altogether, are considered beyond the synagogue's concern. Synagogues propelled to envision anew authorize congregants to take charge of their Jewish lives; professionals move nimbly across boundaries to help each other and to entertain new ideas that none of them independently might have considered.

Extending Space

One ready sign of decentralization is the breakdown of spatial inhibitions. Temple Israel's Riverway project met in people's homes, not in the synagogue; Westchester Reform bought a neighboring building for a retreat center. Temple Micah moved the *Oneg Shabbat* to the beginning of services, and into the gathering area outside the main-floor sanctuary, rather than the social hall downstairs. Activities that stretch across different spaces should be treated holistically, as at Agudath Israel, where Randi Brockman noticed people coming to Friday night services "for the evening... not just for the service." So at the *Oneg*, she directed individuals standing alone to a table of people to talk to.

Space is never absolutely "fixed." Philosopher Hilary Putnam says, "The mind and the world together make up the mind and the world." Visionary congregations free up the mind to partner with the world.

Rescuing the Rabbi

A huge benefit of decentralizing authority is that it frees the rabbi from the burden of being the sole and final determiner of everything. Celia says of her rabbi,

> He can experiment more freely, consult more broadly, and decide more easily what to spend his working time on. The people he works with take much more responsibility and achieve more satisfaction; committees work together (or in Micah's case actually dissolve), in favor of task forces initiated by anyone at all who chooses to activate the web site in favor of a Jewish idea that just might work.

Staff Strains: Hiring and Firing

Change strains old staff arrangements in two ways. The easier and more pleasant of the two is the need to expand professional capacity by new hires. Much more difficult is the challenge of firing, retiring, replacing, or otherwise going around people who may have served in the synagogue for years, but are unable to acclimatize to the new thinking.

If all politics is local, as one-time House Speaker Tip O'Neill remarked, all transformation is local too. The ability to add new people varies with a synagogue's financial means, but also its ability to access local resources. Our synagogue leaders had a feel for their own culture and its surrounding milieu, the "local ecology," as we call it.

Wellesley's Beth Elohim, for example, benefited from already having experienced Boston's *Meah* program, a curriculum of adult study offered at the city's Hebrew College and then localized within individual synagogues. Without help from its Combined Jewish Philanthropy (CJP), *Meah* would have been beyond the financial reach of synagogues. But CJP did help, in part because of its remarkably forward-thinking director, Barry Schrage. But even Barry would have been unable to accomplish what he did without Boston's local specialty: university professors. Similarly, Temple Micah accessed a large pool of talented Washingtonians who work in and around government and politics.

Harder than hiring was firing. Rabbis had to make hard decisions about the professional (and support) team they inherited, letting people go if necessary. Sometimes, those uncomfortable with the change process chose to leave. Sometimes, they had to be fired. David Wentworth at Temple Micah analyzed it well:

> Small not-for-profit institutions, including religious organizations, often ignore the fact that they also have to function as businesses. If they don't successfully manage practical and financial matters, they often cannot function well at their intended purpose. ... Too often, decisions aren't made on a rational basis, they're made for emotional reasons.... At the core, they are all small village entities where everyone knows everyone; it is synagogue as family.

Indeed, most synagogues do operate like families or, at least, like a mom-and-pop store. The staff, the teachers, and even the professionals and clergy may well have been there "forever." Questioning old job descriptions, altering priorities, and pushing people to work outside their comfort zone are apt to be resisted. Especially if the people involved are volunteers, it may appear scandalous to replace them.

Finding Funding

All this costs money, and even congregations with means struggled to raise it. Rabbis usually became fund-raisers. A good example is Temple Israel's Riverway project, which costs $250,000 a year. Senior rabbi Ronne Friedman had to find a donor and fund the project off-budget. Now it is budgeted, the pride of the Temple community. At Beth Am too, says Jim Heeger, "[Rabbi] Rick [Block] did a good job at courting wealthy people" so as to raise the necessary funds—this was in Palo Alto, mind you, a culture that prides itself on understanding the necessity for venture capital, but still needed rabbinic intervention to get it.

Smaller congregations with less wealth adopted other strategies. "We seem to have everybody except very rich people," bemoans Temple Micah's Celia Shapiro, so the religious school was staffed by parents, and when the congregation wanted instruments for its Shabbat services, music director Teddy Klaus formed a pick-up band.

Even while raising money, synagogues in our sample managed to avoid the "4Ms" of *Making Macher Money Matter*. Eddie Reynolds explains "You could not cause a bigger fight at Beth Am than to even suggest that you name something." Beth Elohim too prided itself on not being like their neighbors, where, as they saw it, "The *machers* get the best seats." Celia Shapiro boasts of Micah, "The big *machers* here are the four-year-olds."

Striving for Excellence

All our sample synagogues recognized that synagogues cannot afford mediocrity. Everyone enters a synagogue at one time or another, if only for life-cycle events, and when they arrive, synagogues are, of necessity, on trial. So too were ECE and S2K, which worked because they modeled such excellence. "The ECE program itself was very well run, very, very professional, very thoughtful," recalls Bill Blumstein of Westchester Reform Temple, which participated in ECE and then in S2K. "By the time I was going to Synagogue 2000 meetings," he adds, "I felt like this again.... People whose very first experience was with Synagogue 2000 were blown away, they thought it was so great."

The lesson is clear: both synagogues and intervention programs must be well funded and run with excellence. That means being demanding of people, even the volunteers, all the while maintaining the sense of family, mutuality, and loving concern.

How Change Teams Spoke

Most synagogues report meetings given over to run-of-the-mill reports, tedious agendas, and mundane problems—an unhappy bar-mitzvah family or a leaky roof. Board members complain that their meetings are either tediously unproductive (they should be more business-like) or lacking in spiritual satisfaction (they should be less business-like). The congregations we studied managed to get beyond that. On fire with the joy of learning, experimenting, and even praying, together, they developed a think-tank atmosphere, asking big questions and proposing equally big solutions. They discovered a *new kind of conversation*. Behind that conversation was successful *encoding* and *enstorying*.

Encoding the Present

We often say of what is new, "Words fail us," meaning we have no appropriate verbal code to express our thoughts. But in order to *act* differently, congregations must also *speak* differently. That is called "*encoding* our experience." We therefore tracked how congregations described what they were trying to do.

But visionary synagogues question not just *what they do* but *what they are*. We distinguish, therefore, between *activity* and *identity*. What an institution does and the spirit with which it does it provide its identity (a social-action synagogue, a place for kids, and so on). When people choose to act out their lives within a synagogue, they identify with that identity. People who join a congregation of learners or a sacred community identify differently from those who just drop off kids for bar/bat mitzvah training, or who go intermittently to this or that lecture as a way to spend an interesting evening.

Once, our identity was given at birth—a heritage of religion, race, class, and sex. Today, we often have a say in these things. From characters in a novel that someone else wrote, we have become authors of our own stories, and the story we call our own constitutes what philosopher Charles Taylor calls our "moral space." People *belong* to functional congregations, the way they *belong* to health clubs and frequent-flyer programs. People *identify* with visionary synagogues; they throw in their lot with what the synagogue *is*, rather than show up briefly for what the synagogue *does*.

What language did our visionary congregations use to express what they thought it worthwhile to *be*?

To begin with, they overwhelmingly used words of *joy*. They recall their childhood synagogue education as anywhere from painful to useless. They were made to feel guilty for all their "nots": not attending services, not knowing enough, and not keeping Halakhah. Rabbis were distant, pontificating, and foreboding. Jewish history was an exercise in persecution and tribulation. Visionary synagogues promise joy instead of sadness; worth instead of guilt.

We also encountered words like "deliberate," "intentional," and "passionate." Respondents wanted "to share," and "to search." They were on a "journey," locating "portals" and "gateways" to "experiences" that would prove "meaningful" and "fun." Much like the nineteenth century, our era can be labeled "romantic," in that it promotes feeling over logic. Unless prompted, our respondents rarely spoke conceptually of Jewish Peoplehood, God, Torah, or Israel. With few exceptions we heard little thought-through theology. More often, the goal was self-realization. Melissa Kelly of Beth Am is an example: "It was everything that I felt lacking in the synagogue of my youth—the genuine warmth of community, meaningful Jewish study, worship that is relevant to my life, and silly fun—lots of it." So too is Nancy Belsky: "It was really kind of fun to watch the joy people get out of religion, which I never quite got. It became a very warm cozy place to be Friday night…. I feel good. I like to spend my time in a place that feels good."

"Meaningfulness" is paramount. Rick Jacobs spoke for many when he said, "You don't get points for being a *big* congregation. You only get points for being a *meaningful* congregation." "Meaningful" testifies to a felt connection between the synagogue and the personal growth stories of the congregants, evidence again of our romanticized passion for what Robert Bellah has called "expressive individualism." We yearn to express who we, uniquely, are, using what sociologists (and ordinary Americans too) call "style," the almost limitless ways we dress, outfit our homes, and pursue experiences that are "the real us." When we think we have captured that essence, says Charles Taylor, we call it "authentic." We expect the institutions we frequent to support our self-expression as the "authentic" persons we think we are. That is, in part, what we mean by "meaningful."

But only "in part." Authentic selves need authentic roots in an equally authentic past, hence the overwhelming popularity of text study, from which informants extract traditional wording to characterize their activities. Angela Buchdahl says of her temple's *tzedakah* collection, "We thought we'd actually have built-in collection areas in the four corners of the room. It's like *pe'ah* in the four corners, to provide for those with need, in dignity." Hebrew titles that congregants would not use otherwise, and that most of them cannot even translate, function symbolically to announce Jewish authenticity: *neshamah Shabbat, chavayah* (a high school program), *ohel tzedek* (for social justice), and assorted programs entitled *morashah, tzavta,* and *mercaz.*

Language need not always be traditional, however. It is sometimes just a memorable one-liner that a congregational change team found catchy. "If it ain't broke, break it," was Temple Micah's watchword; Jenny Oser uses the language of speed dating to define her for social-justice organizing as "speed one-on-ones." "We do Shabbas," says Paula Mack Drill. Rabbi Jonah Pesner comments, "We are a *tzedek* congregation." These pet slogans are "cheers" says Rick Jacobs, "ways for the team to be cheerleaders for the next incarnation of Judaism."

Enstorying the Past

Identity is not just a momentary thing, however; it stretches through time, against a backdrop of what we think we have been. The book of our lives must be authored, chapter by chapter, with a plot line that follows a believable trajectory. As *communal* selves in change, synagogues plot their next chapter, needing something sufficiently new to be "transformative," but not so revolutionary as to constitute a completely new self. So our change teams did not just encode their present; they also *enstoried* their past.

By that, we mean that synagogues remained true to their story—even to the extent of not crediting outside interventions too much, for fear of sounding as if they were betraying their own internal authenticity. At Westchester Reform, for instance, Peter Wang knows "the real engine driving this [the on-campus "retreat center" that the congregation built] ... reverts back to the ECE roots as ultimately nourished by Synagogue 2000." But "We didn't want to hear 'another ECE,' or 'S2K'.... so we called it WRT 2000." Josh Seidman at Temple Micah is even clearer: "I don't know if you know the term NIH – 'not invented here.' We were trying to do things and were very conscious that a lot of this was Synagogue 2000.... We were trying to figure out ways to implement them without called anything Synagogue 2000."

Enstorying is the way we fit new chapters to the old story; and the decision to move from functional to visionary is such a chapter.

Going Deeper: Deep-rooting the Change

If synagogues were merely utilitarian—the religious equivalent of stores that offer merchandise, or factories that manufacture goods—

we would be content with congregations that are "functional." But visionary synagogues hold themselves accountable to a higher goal. Think of synagogues, then, as institutions dedicated to such things as making the world a better place (*tikkun olam*), acting as God wants us to (performing *mitzvot*), informing life's search for meaning (Torah study), and the like. Most synagogues pay lip service to these overarching values, but because they are merely functional they have only limited success in achieving them.

The Talmud addresses such failure by asking *ma'i m'akev*, "what gets in the way?" So *ma'i m'akev* when it comes to synagogues? The answer is: infrastructural systems that protect the status quo, like defense mechanisms that individuals erect to resist therapeutic correction of personality defects. If these are not addressed, the synagogue will eventually revert to its default position: mere functionality.

Institutions, like individuals, prefer to deny self-destructive behavior rather than face up to it. Meanwhile, damage metastasizes. Personal gains squeeze out public well-being; honest evaluation of human resources declines; insecure professionals protect themselves by scapegoating each other; misunderstandings are papered over and allowed to fester until they explode; transparency disappears; efficiency declines; healthy public debate deteriorates into insidious off-line conversation. Transformative synagogues face up to these systemic fault lines. How do they do it?

Corporatism or Charisma?

One way to chart attention to systemic change is to think about the interrelationship between corporatism and charisma. By corporate we mean simply the normative structure of committees, due process, and board regulations. Some synagogues abide only loosely by such standards. Others are rich in structural density. On the other side of things is rabbinic charisma, the extent to which rabbis act outside the normative corporate channels. On the face of it, corporate structure discourages personal charisma, while personal charisma resents being hemmed in by committees and rules. How do corporate mentality, on the one hand, and personal charisma, on the other, handle systemic change? We devised scales of corporatism and of charisma to answer that question.

In sum, congregations varied widely on both. At one extreme on the corporation scale was Beth Am, where long-term member Mel Kronick remembers the "early years when the strong lay leadership of Eddie Reynolds brought into the congregation ... a lot of collaborative institutionalized ways of running committees and strategic focus groups." Over time, some people feared that "the congregation was becoming too corporate." But it fit the style of the then rabbi, Rick Block; and his successor, Rabbi Janet Marder, who says she was "impressed by the organizational culture," used it to make change happen.

At the other extreme is Temple Micah, where committees were so weak that the rabbi (Danny Zemel) was able to demolish them. "I hated going to committee meetings and I discovered that everybody else pretty much hated going to committee meetings," Danny explains. "For sure, nobody misses the social action committee and we have a lot more social action than we ever had with the committee."

Pioneering sociologist Max Weber famously distinguished authority as charismatic, traditional, or rational/legal. Charisma works through individual magnetism (John F. Kennedy or Winston Churchill); tradition depends on established right of rule (royalty passes from father to oldest son); rational/legal authority depends on roles within systems (even a corporate president is restrained by regulations and structure). Like democratic leadership in general, all our synagogues operated with at least a modicum of rational/legal authority; all the rabbis worked within some degree of corporate boundary-setting. But even congregations high on the corporate scale overcame bureaucratic excess, and used their corporate structure to address systemic dysfunction.

What about charisma? By charisma we mean something other than the simplified model of a popular "pied piper" attracting the masses through personal "star power." We also mean something other than the traditional Chasidic *tzaddik*, often a charismatic figure, but also the *traditional* inheritor of the family right to leadership. We have in mind what we call *soft charisma*, charisma that did not come by virtue of flashy or compelling personality. This was charisma that the rabbis earned by virtue of their character, their mastery of Jewish wisdom, and their will to build trusting relationships with lay partners. In sociological terms, their charisma was attained, but it was not automatic.

Some of our leaders did demonstrate innate pied-piper ability, but they too had to earn respect, and what mattered in the end was the "soft charismatic" combination of *learning, relationship,* and *character*. All our rabbis scored high on that charisma scale.

Cultures were transformed either because the corporate hierarchy worked efficiently to achieve it, or because charismatic rabbis constantly demanded it, or, usually, a combination of both. Above all, it took perseverance—insistence over time that the congregation's new chapter was indeed going to get written.

It is too early to know if the changes will prove long-lasting, but we have good reason to believe that at least in some of the places we studied it will. In the meantime, the process of congregational transformation is no longer a matter of speculation. We know a good deal about how it occurs.

Notes

1. Adapted from I. Aron, S.M. Cohen, L. Hoffman and A.Y. Kelman, *Sacred Strategies: Transforming Functional Synagogues into Visionary Congregations* (Woodstock, Vt.: Jewish Lights Publishing, forthcoming, 2009). The author would like to thank the following federations, foundation, and individuals for their generous support of the research that informs this article: The Commission on Jewish Identity and Renewal of UJA-Federation of New York; The Nathan Cummings Foundation; The Combined Jewish Philanthropies of Boston; Mr. Arthur Winn; and The Esther F. and William J. Bushman Beth Shalom Endowment Fund of the Jewish Community Foundation of Greater Kansas City.

Keeping the Mice in Shul: Principles for Synagogue Transformation

Richard J. Jacobs

Recently a visitor came up to me after services and insisted on telling me an old joke: "A church and a synagogue are next to each other. One day the priest tells the rabbi, 'We're having a terrible problem with mice in the church. We've tried everything but we can't seem to get rid of the little vermin.' The priest then asks the rabbi, 'I heard you don't have a problem with mice. Could you tell me how you do it?' The rabbi answers: 'Well, it's really rather easy. We *bar mitzvah* the mice. After they become *bar mitzvah*, they leave the synagogue and never come back." The joke makes many people laugh; it makes others of us cry, and a few just don't get it, at least not anymore.

Rather than laugh or cry at this tired joke, many congregations, including ours, have been busy transforming into Jewish communities of depth and engagement. Since the early 1990s, The Experiment in Congregational Education (ECE), Synagogue 2000/3000 (S2K/S3K), and Synagogue Transformation and Renewal (STAR) have worked hard changing synagogues for the better. Some insist that the era of synagogue transformation is over, but I hope they are wrong. Synagogue transformation is so much more than attending a URJ biennial workshop or probing the subject at a day-long board retreat, catalyzing as those may be. At Westchester Reform Temple (WRT) we have spent the last fourteen years working with ECE and S2K/S3K to retool our congregation to better meet the challenges of Jewish life. The gurus of synagogue transformation, Isa Aron, Sara Lee, Larry Hoffman, and Ron Wolfson, have provoked us to think differently about every aspect of temple life and have inspired many improvements and changes. Only now are we finally getting to the

RICHARD J. JACOBS (NY82) is rabbi of Westchester Reform Temple in Scarsdale, New York.

deeper, systemic change following years of harvesting the proverbial "low-hanging fruit." It's not that we were a dysfunctional synagogue. Quite the contrary. But even with our strengths, the challenges of real Jewish engagement were eluding too many of our
members.

The following are principles that have guided our work at WRT
over these past fourteen years. I share them with the hope that they
may prove helpful to others at various stages of synagogue growth
and change.

1. Tell the truth

This is a deceptively simple practice. When Ed Koch was mayor of
New York, he asked everyone he met, "How am I doing?" The
response depended upon whom he asked. And how are we doing?
Reform Judaism is the largest movement in American Jewish life.
We have hundreds of well-run, active synagogues; we have lots of
bright and talented rabbis, cantors, and educators; but we don't
have to look too closely to see that most of our temple religious
schools produce graduates who are functionally illiterate in Judaism. How many of our adult education programs offer more than
introductory surveys of Judaism? How many of our boards of trustees spend inordinate amounts of time debating whether or not to fix
the roof or the heating system rather than figure out new ways to
animate the synagogue with Judaism? Synagogue change stops the
moment we stop telling the truth about our institutions.

2. First things first

Synagogue change can't tackle areas of congregational life ran-
domly; the sequence matters. For WRT that meant beginning with
learning programs and not worship or sacred community. Religious school was failing not because we had a bad one, but rather
because the model of supplementary schools is broken. The synagogue school too often resembles a Jewish children's gas station
with parents dropping their kids off to be picked up two hours later
with the expectation that they will be filled with Jewish knowledge
and commitment. This model is deeply flawed. Few people argued
that religious school was so meaningful that it ought not to be
changed. There is much less resistance to changing something that
most people agree is not functioning well. With worship, many
congregants are strongly attached to the status quo, however unin-

spiring it may be to the next generation. If we had begun with our synagogue transformation by taking on worship change, I doubt we would have gotten very far. Other synagogue cultures might require that the transformation work begin with social action or with sacred community. Knowing where to begin is an exercise in knowing the culture of the congregation. There are so many things that need to change, but "first things first."

3. Never say *"dayeinu"*
("It would have been enough")

Quitting too soon is the most common mistake of all synagogue change initiatives. **If only** we can increase participation in adult learning, *dayeinu*. **If only** we retain more *b'nei mitzvah* students for continuing Jewish learning, *dayeinu*. Synagogue professionals are usually too busy to sustain long-term change initiatives. So we call it quits prematurely. Twelve years ago, we piloted a new model called Sharing Shabbat, which requires families to come weekly for Shabbat worship, study, and community. For us the *dayeinu* moment might have been when twenty-five percent of families in our religious school chose to make that commitment. But instead of quitting while we were ahead, we pushed further by applying what we learned from our pilot to all of our religious school learning. Had we stopped earlier it **would not** have been enough.

4. "Ready, fire, aim!"

The fourth principle is counterintuitive, yet it is the key: "Ready, fire, aim!" We have all been taught to put these steps in the correct order: Ready, aim, fire. Too often synagogues begin with a comprehensive strategic plan that requires ten years of research and meetings. This thinking demands that we figure out beforehand exactly what steps need to be taken in order to reach the Promised Land. Unfortunately, by the time we finish the strategic study we are almost sure to have missed the moving target. "Ready, fire, aim" puts us into a culture of experimentation: try it, innovate, learn, refine, and retry. For us, we have convinced our community that only through experimentation will we one day get it right.

A number of years ago, we experimented by having two different Friday night services each week. The early service was shorter with participatory music, contemporary liturgy, and a brief *d'var Torah*. The later service had the feel of classical Reform Judaism, with the choice of majestic music, more formal liturgical choreography, and a traditional sermon. When we announced this experiment (after a year and a half of study by our worship task force), we didn't declare, "Here's the new Torah from Sinai." Instead, we told our community that we were going to try some new approaches, but that there would be plenty of opportunity for congregational feedback and refinement. The push back was reduced because we didn't present the initiative as a *fait accompli.* "Ready, fire, aim" has served us well.

5. Be bold without bulldozing

This is easier said than done. Seventeen years ago my wife and I bought an old house and, as we were fixing it up, the previous owners showed up and walked through. They couldn't believe how we were "ruining" what they thought was a gorgeous house. I like to describe effective synagogue transformation as renovating our congregation's life while the long-time members continue living happily in our midst. Throughout our efforts at synagogue change, we have tried to imagine "previous owners" watching every change without blocking all creative efforts. Long-time members were specifically invited to be part of our reimagining work groups with the belief that diverse views are essential to success. We've learned that you can't legislate what matters. You can plant seeds and use more carrots than sticks to point the way ahead. We have found that over time folks buy into bold changes if they are not bulldozed into accepting them.

6. Raising the bar won't drive people away

The sixth principle flows directly from the fifth. It's a limiting assumption of synagogue life that raising the bar will drive people away, whether the bar is learning, observance, commitment to *tikkun olam,* or sense of responsibility to the community. Yes, our board of trustees worries about the same things that many other boards worry about and that is "Will we get new members if we keep raising the bar?" Among our 850 religious school students, we no longer have parents just dropping off their little ones to get filled with Jewish studies. New-member families are now expected to come in for study, prayer, and acts of *tikkun olam.* With this expectation, will the folks continue to join? So far we have found that raising the bar has not turned people away. Less isn't always more; in fact, most often less is less when it comes to congregational norms. The key is how the bar is raised.

Transformation takes a lot of time, whereas changes occur quickly. We are only now getting to the proverbial "high-hanging fruit" of synagogue change, the deeper cultural change. We are in the midst of building a new campus because our practice of Judaism has changed. Now we need our spiritual home to reflect those changes. Our Jewish learning no longer fits into religious school classrooms but rather requires a new *beit midrash* with multiple seminar rooms along with large spaces for informal Jewish learning for our students of all ages. And with new modalities of worship, we no longer fit into our post-WWII sanctuary.

A few years back, a woman who had been an active lay leader wanted to meet to talk about worship at the temple. I knew she was from a classical Reform background, so I was nervous about the meeting because I knew she wasn't fulfilled with our ritual experiments. "I hate all the worship changes," she told me. "But I came to Sharing Shabbat with my grandson, and now I get what is going on. I don't love it. It's not for me, but I saw the light in my grandson's eyes, and now I won't stand in the way as I had before." She understood what was behind the changes. This was one of the best moments of my rabbinate. She confirmed that we were on the right road to our Jewish future.

A Word on Partnerships for Transformation

There is no single blueprint for synagogue change, but the transformation projects and the growing body of research have been invaluable to our modest efforts. Our task forces and board have studied Lawrence Hoffman's *ReThinking Synagogues*, Ron Wolfson's *The Spirituality of Welcome*, and Isa Aron's *The Self-Renewing Congregation* to name just a few of the recent books that provide new thinking to inspire innovative practice in leading the congregations of the twenty-first century.

Synagogue change has been aided by visionary funders who have understood the necessity and value of providing grants to bold experiments in doing synagogue differently. I remember when we received a UJA-Federation of New York grant to redesign our high school education program. Some must have questioned giving a grant to a congregation in Scarsdale. Such grants can be crucial not because our communities are impoverished but rather because the endorsement of respected funders can convince lay leaders and members to value the initiative even more.

None of us can transform synagogues without partners. ECE, S3K, STAR, Just Congregations, The Institute for Jewish Spirituality, and local federations have expertise, change strategies, mentoring, and financial support to help retool our congregations for the twenty-first century.

Whenever a congregation undertakes a journey of change, there is always much more that can be done to get closer to that elusive Promised Land. It is my prayer that the transformation projects will find new ways to catalyze more thoughtful experimentation in the core areas of synagogue life. We are presently rethinking what our professional team portfolios should be in light of past changes and a future vision. There is still a great need for wise consultants to help birth these changes. The Jewish community has had a very short attention span when it comes to sustaining change in synagogues, but our children and grandchildren deserve better than what we have been able to do to date. The journey of change in synagogues from good to great is surely filled with peaks and valleys. But as we know from the end of Deuteronomy, we are forever "on the way."

I conclude with a quote from Charles Darwin, the man who spent his life trying to understand the nature of change. "It is not the strongest of the species that survives nor the most intelligent, but the one most responsive to change." *Kein y'hi ratzon* for all of our synagogues.

Bibliography

Aron, Isa. *Becoming a Congregation of Learners: Learning as a Key to Revitalizing Congregational Life*, Vt.: Jewish Lights, 2000.

——————. *The Self-Renewing Congregation: Organizational Strategies for Revitalizing Congregational Life*, Vt.: Jewish Lights, 2002.

Aron, Isa, et al., eds., *A Congregation of Learners: Transforming the Synagogue into a Learning Community*, N.Y.: UAHC Press, 1995.

Hoffman, Lawrence A. *ReThinking Synagogues: A New Vocabulary for Congregational Life*, Woodstock, Vt.: Jewish Lights, 2006.

Wolfson, Ron. *The Spirituality of Welcoming: How to Transform Your Congregation into a Sacred Community*, Vt.: Jewish Lights, 2006.

The Riverway Project
Engaging Adults in Their 20s and 30s in the Process of Transforming the Synagogue

Jeremy S. Morrison

In the spring of 2007, Synagogue 3000 published an article written by Tobin Belzer and Donald E. Miller titled, "Synagogues that Get It: How Jewish Congregations are Engaging Young Adults."[1] In their study, Belzer and Miller described three synagogues—in L.A., Chicago, and New York City—that are "making a concerted effort to understand and engage young adults by proactively addressing young adults' multi-faceted interests in religion."[2] Belzer and Miller note that presently the majority of individuals in their twenties and thirties have no congregational affiliation, and that their affiliation rate is lower than that of any other age cohort.[3] Moreover, congregations have been slow to adapt themselves to effectively addressing the needs of this demographic group.

The present article is a description of another synagogue that, to borrow Belzer and Miller's phrase, "gets it." Temple Israel of Boston is the home of the Riverway Project (RWP). Named after the location of Temple Israel, the RWP is an outreach and engagement initiative for those in their twenties and thirties living in metropolitan Boston. The RWP seeks to connect greater numbers of adults in their twenties and thirties to Judaism and to the synagogue through a variety of entry-points. Launched in the spring of 2001, the RWP has succeeded at engaging this age cohort in synagogue communal life.

What follows is a discussion of the RWP's history and its methods for engaging twenties and thirties in the process of creating meaningful Jewish experiences. Furthermore, this article will describe how the RWP's approach to organizing and to perpetuating itself has begun to transform Temple Israel, a 1600-member, 155-year-old, urban congregation.[4]

JEREMY S. MORRISON (NY01) is a rabbi of Temple Israel in Boston, Massachusetts.

The Learning Curve: Moving from Place to People

In my fourth year of rabbinical school, I proposed to the clergy of Temple Israel the idea of opening a satellite of the Temple—a kind of storefront synagogue for adults in their twenties and thirties—in the South End of Boston, a gentrifying, urban neighborhood that is the home to many in this demographic. My approaching Temple Israel with this concept was no accident. I had grown up in the congregation, was very familiar with its entrepreneurial and innovative methods for constructing a synagogue community, and had maintained a close relationship with its senior rabbi, Ronne Friedman.

At that time in the South End, which was, incidentally, where Temple Israel had had its first sanctuary (now an AME Zion Church), there was no established liberal, Jewish presence. Our initial vision (which we called, "An Extension of Israel") focused on creating a space that would serve the needs of this disengaged population. The storefront's various activities would have complemented what was already occurring at the main Temple Israel building (for instance, we would not have had programs for young children, nor high holy day services) and would easily be interwoven into the lives of urban Jews.

This emphasis on creating a physical space for activities was one of our early stumbles. A task force created by the Board of the synagogue to analyze the financial implications of this endeavor determined that this undertaking would be too expensive, and an entanglement of both financial and legal issues rendered this first iteration of our vision as infeasible. However, this stumble ultimately served us, because it motivated us to shift our focus from creating a space to forging relationships among people (see below). Furthermore, this evolution produced several of the core and lasting ingredients of RWP's success.

Along these lines, we "broke ground" for the RWP by organizing a series of house meetings in the late spring of 2001. We met with unaffiliated Jews living in several neighborhoods in which we now have established circles for Jewish activities, and we asked the participants about their connections to Judaism, their reluctance to become affiliated with a synagogue, what of Judaism they would like to try, where they would like to try it, what we could do to help, and similar questions. Participants responded that they were seeking Shabbat meals and services in an intimate setting, serious learning about Judaism, and social action projects. They wanted to start with activities in their own neighborhoods, and they sought a mix of ages and types (e.g., married and single, older and younger; interfaith couples) to join together. Additionally, participants wanted any social connections to flow from these activities, rather than focusing on the social or dating aspect. Many found it awkward to go to events with the goal of meeting a partner and found it off-putting to go "cold" into a large synagogue. Out of these stated interests and concerns, the initial content of the RWP's initiatives emerged. To this day, our participants' desires continue to direct all our programming, and the intimate setting of people's living-rooms continues to be instrumental in forging relationships.

Later in 2001, with a donor-funded, one-year contract, but without any significant dollars to spend on programming, my wife and I moved to the South End, where we had found an apartment with a living-room large enough to hold services and communal meals. In that first year we conducted twenty-seven gatherings in five Boston neighborhoods, an effort that built the foundation for the growth of the project. In some ways, we were able to reincorporate our initial vision: RWP events that occur outside of Temple Israel's building but happen in participants' neighborhoods and living-rooms are considered an "extension" of Temple Israel, and all our programming is conducted at times and in places that are conducive to the busy, work-filled lives of our participants. And a couple of times each year we use a donated storefront in the South End as a space for *Kabbalat Shabbat* services.

Meaningful Judaism

The RWP is comprised of worship, study, and social justice activities conducted both within Temple Israel's building and in various locations throughout the Boston metropolitan area. In an attempt to engage unaffiliated Jews in the creation of Jewish community in both informal and institutional settings, the RWP provides a panoply of connecting points, including casual Shabbat experiences in participants' homes, low-cost opportunities to join this urban congregation formally, and regular opportunities for Torah study.[5] On average, there are four to six RWP gatherings each month.

A hallmark of the RWP is a network of neighborhood circles situated in four urban areas in and around Boston. The circles meet in homes for *Shabbat* meals or services, study sessions, or *Havdalah*.

Although the circles are designed to be a tool for creating communities of Jews living in a particular neighborhood, the activities of each circle are open to anyone in their twenties and thirties living in Boston. Consequently, at each event there are participants from different parts of the city, and the circles serve to form a wide network of qualitative relationships among our target population. Each circle has twelve to eighteen core members. Often partnering with aspiring guitarists and text teachers, I frequently lead the *Kabbalat Shabbat* services within the circles, while, with the aid of a coordinator, the participants organize and lead their own Shabbat dinners and other study and ritual gatherings.

In conjunction with RWP programming around the city, the RWP also holds programs at Temple Israel designed to introduce participants to synagogue life and to integrate them into the larger Temple Israel community. These activities include holiday celebrations; study sessions; social action initiatives; "Riverway Tots" (a bi-weekly, pre-Shabbat experience for parents with children up to three years old); and "Soul Food Fridays" (a monthly Friday night service at Temple Israel solely for those in their twenties and thirties).

In addition to our emphasis on partnership and ownership, a serious and critical approach to text-study is one of the RWP's main methods for connecting adults in their twenties and thirties to each other, to Temple Israel, and to Judaism. Over time, we have developed stratified learning opportunities.[6] We began with a program that continues today: "Torah and Tonics on Tuesday," a bi-monthly opportunity to study the Torah portion of the week at the Temple. No Hebrew or prior knowledge is required for this drop-in learning experience. Building on our participants' increased comfort with and interest in study, we created a neighborhood-based educational experience called "Mining for Meaning." "Mining" is a four-session course designed to deepen RWP participants' understanding of Jewish rituals, their function in one's life, and their origin. Each session includes in-depth text study to elucidate the historical roots of particular rituals, as well as a "how to" workshop (demonstrations and discussions on adapting certain rituals to one's life). Most recently, in partnership with the Combined Jewish Philanthropies and Hebrew College, we offered a new model of *Me'ah*, designed for this age group and taught by instructors in their thirties.[7]

The People

The population of RWP participants is heterogeneous. The majority is over the age of 25. The range of professional pursuits is vast, including artists, graduate students, entrepreneurs, architects, teachers, doctors, and lawyers. Approximately 50% of participants are married or in ongoing relationships; about 25% of the participants are in interfaith relationships. A growing percentage of participants have infants or toddlers. For many, the RWP is either his or her first encounter with organized Jewish activity or marks a return to Jewish communal life after a hiatus that began when the participant left home for college. If a participant's family was affiliated with a synagogue during his or her childhood, it was most likely Reform. Roughly 15% of participants describe their Jewish background as Conservative, Reconstructionist, Humanistic, or secular, and an estimated 2% of RWP participants report that they are from Orthodox homes. What unifies most RWP participants is a low level of Jewish knowledge and a beginner's experience of Jewish ritual. Few have studied Jewish texts before engaging with the RWP; most have only a rudimentary or no understanding of Hebrew.[8]

The RWP has connected with a sizeable, diverse, and dynamic group of adults in their twenties and thirties. Approximately 1,500 people have, to varying degrees, affiliated with RWP programming. Several hundred have become members of Temple Israel. However, as would be expected in any large catchment of adults in this age-group, the RWP's population is always in transition. After three to five years many of our core participants either move to new cities or become engaged with the synagogue in new ways as they grow older, have children, and assume roles as participants or leaders in the larger Temple Israel community. Consequently, the RWP is constantly in the process of renewing its "base" by building relationships with new participants and developing new leaders. Ideally, the RWP—and the synagogue as a whole—is continually in a process of transformation: we seek to adapt our methods, structures, and programs to ensure that they are consistent with both Jewish tradition and the ever-changing ideas and lives of the members of our community.

Engendering Ownership

Since the RWP's inception, we have sought to create leadership opportunities consistent with the quest for Jewish meaning that motivates most of the RWP participants. Rather than replicating the leadership models of many synagogues with fixed committees that oversee various types of programs (e.g., the ritual committee, the education committee) we have, instead, fostered a relational model of partnership between professionals and participants—and among the participants themselves—engaging all who are interested in the process of creating authentic Jewish experiences.

For example, one of the goals of the "Mining" experience is to create ongoing, self-sustaining learning circles (what we are now calling "Still Mining for Meaning") with participants becoming confident teachers of text for one another. In different neighborhoods participants have continued to study theology, liturgy, and *parashat hashavuah* together. Typically, each monthly session is taught by a member of the circle who, beforehand, meets with me or with a colleague to prepare a lesson plan. Furthermore, these gatherings are organized around the ritual of *Havdalah*, which also is led by the participants.

Two years ago, we created an ever-changing leadership group of twenty to twenty-five core participants that meets quarterly to evaluate, brainstorm, and plan. This group does not function as an advisory committee or focus group. Rather, to be part of this leadership "team" means to be an owner of RWP experiences. By initiating new activities and improving current ones, this group of leaders is deeply involved in strengthening the RWP community. They are visionaries, as well as implementers, who serve as the hosts, greeters, teachers, and musicians at RWP gatherings.

The coordinator of the RWP and I serve as organizers who facilitate connections between the participants based on common interests. As the founder of the RWP, I developed a model and infrastructure for building Jewish community within this cohort. However, determining the content of RWP gatherings is a joint effort. What I teach as a rabbi in the community, when I teach, and how Judaism is taught emerges through dialogue with the participants. And the few times early on, when we created programs not initiated through collaboration, they didn't succeed.[9]

Synagogue Transformation

The presence of a sizeable and growing population of adults in their twenties and thirties has brought new energy and enthusiasm into the synagogue, and the RWP is serving as a model within the larger Temple Israel community for adding depth and quality to the Jewish life of its members. Importantly, the inception of the RWP coincided with the commencement of our social justice initiative known as *Ohel Tzedek* (Tent of Justice). Both of these endeavors are premised on relational-based models of organizing, and together the RWP and *Ohel Tzedek* have profoundly altered how Temple Israel transforms itself. Our interfaith, new member, and adult education activities are now developed through the methods that we utilize in the RWP. Slowly, Temple Israel is becoming a synagogue community comprised of qualitative relationships among its participants.

Although the present iteration of the RWP is less expensive than what we originally proposed, generating financial support continues to be a challenge. As might be assumed, the greatest expense of the project is my salary and benefits. But as I have explained to other synagogue leaders who have inquired about how we built the RWP, congregations do not need to hire a new member of the clergy to lead this kind of initiative. Instead, what is required is a re-prioritization of how a rabbi or cantor spends his or her time. The funds that we have raised to support the RWP have been, obviously, crucial to the development of this idea. But equally valuable to the success of the RWP was (and is) the synagogue's shift in priorities. The leadership of Temple Israel understands that this kind of outreach to twenties and thirties is vital to the perpetuation of the synagogue.[10]

In the past decade, many independent *minyanim*, comprised of Jews in their twenties and thirties, have emerged as a response, in part, to synagogues that "don't get it." But Temple Israel does. Its leadership has learned that relational methods for transforming the synagogue can be powerfully effective in this moment of Jewish history. By developing meaningful pathways for connecting with Judaism, the RWP has engaged several hundred adults in their twenties and thirties in this dynamic and creative process. The Riverway Project has transformed their conceptions of the synagogue experience and, I hope, will ensure that these previously disengaged adults will seek out Jewish community throughout the course of their lives.[11]

Notes

1. See Tobin Belzer and Donald E. Miller, "Synagogues that Get It: How Jewish Congregations," S3K Reports 2 (Spring 2007), Synagogue 3000/ S3K Synagogue Studies Institute.

2. See Belzer and Miller, p. 2.

3. Ibid.

4. It is important to note that a practitioner and not a theoretician wrote this article. I have been the director of the Riverway Project since its beginning and therefore I am not in a position to compare the RWP to other outreach efforts by synagogues in other cities. Fortunately, there is a growing body of literature that provides more objective and broader insight regarding this age cohort, its relationship with Judaism, national efforts to connect twenties and thirties to Jewish communal life, and even an academic's study of the RWP itself. See, for instance, Jacob B. Ukeles, Ron Miller, and Pearl Buck, *Young Jewish Adults in the United States Today* (New York: American Jewish Committee, 2007). Also see Beth Cousens, "Shifting Social Networks: Studying the Jewish Growth of Adults in Their Twenties and Thirties" (Ph.D. dissertation, Brandeis University, 2008).

5. All the RWP programs are free or cost the participant $7 to $25. One does not need to be a member of Temple of Israel to participate in RWP programming. However, demonstrating its commitment to adults in their twenties and thirties, Temple Israel has established an introductory, one-year membership of $36/$72 per couple for those 35 years old and under.

6. For a further discussion of Torah and Tonics on Tuesday and the RWP's approach to study, see Beth Cousens, Jeremy S. Morrison, and Susan P. Fendricks, "Using the Contextual Orientation to Facilitate the Study of Bible with Generation X," *Journal of Jewish Education* 74/1(2008), pp. 6–28.

7. Meah is 100 hours of study, at a college level, of Jewish history and text taught by academics and sponsored by Hebrew College and the Combined Jewish Philanthropies.

8. See Cousens, Morrison, and Fendricks, p. 8.

9. For instance, in the first year of the project we held a film festival (in collaboration with the Boston Film Festival) that drew very few participants. A key to our success has been to "mine our niche," offering only programs that deal with ritual, study, or social justice.

10. Here are a few statistics about the RWP and its success:
    - 5 Riverway Project participants have served on Temple Israel's Board of Trustees.
    - Presently, four Riverway Project participants are leaders of Temple Israel's Social Justice initiative (Ohel Tzedek).
    - 22 Riverway Project participants send (or have sent) their children to the pre-school.

- Each month there are 4 to 6 Riverway Project gatherings for study and ritual.
- Each year, for the past 7 years, between 150 and 200 individuals join the synagogue through the Riverway Project.
- 16% of Temple Israel's current membership has joined through the Riverway Project.
- 200 adults in their twenties and thirties attend Soul Food Friday services each month.
- 75 Riverway participants have hosted in their homes Shabbat services, potluck dinners, holiday celebrations, or study sessions.
- 20 Riverway participants have led their peers in text study.
- 14 Riverway participants went on a joint trip to Israel in 2005.
- Six Riverway participants have helped to lead a Shabbat service.
- Five former Riverway Project participants are now at Hebrew Union College as cantorial and rabbinical students.

11. I am grateful to Bethie Miller, the coordinator of outreach and engagement initiatives at Temple Israel, for her thoughtful comments during the preparation of this article.

Temple Emanuel of Beverly Hills:
A Work in Progress

Laura Geller

I didn't set out to transform our synagogue by creating an alternative Shabbat morning minyan. I only wanted a place to pray. I knew
that the ultimate measure of the success of my congregational
rabbinate would be if I could pray in my own synagogue.

When I came to Temple Emanuel of Beverly Hills in 1994, it was
a congregation in distress. It was close to $5,000,000 in debt; the
previous senior rabbi had left; tension between the day school and
the synagogue was toxic; and it was about to be acquired by another
major congregation in what was called a merger. The Board of Directors of both synagogues favored the merger, as did the rabbis,
including the emeritus rabbi of Emanuel, who was called back into
service when the senior rabbi left. Everyone assumed the merger
was a "done deal" until a congregational meeting, when the merger
was defeated by less than fifty votes.

When Emanuel chose me to be the senior rabbi, the leadership was
taking a risk. Although I had been a rabbi for 18 years (serving as the
Hillel director of USC for 14 years and the director of the Pacific South-
west Region of the American Jewish Congress for 4), I had not had a
day of congregational experience. It was less of a risk for me. As Rabbi
Lenny Thal advised me: "If you succeed, it will be your success; if you
fail, everyone will assume it was an impossible job."

For the first several years, I served as the only rabbi. Our bar and
bat mitzvah services, while lovely, were essentially private family
celebrations as opposed to communal worship. The congregation
was too big for everyone to know each other's children and therefore
want to participate in a service led by a thirteen-year-old, however
well trained. So it was clear we needed to create an alternative Shabbat morning experience. My hope at the beginning was that this
alternative service would be a model for what prayer at its best could

LAURA GELLER (NY76) is senior rabbi of Temple Emanuel, Beverly Hills, California.

be and that it would begin to influence the other worship experiences in the congregation.

I was fortunate to be able to hire two incredibly talented rabbis in Los Angeles who didn't have Shabbat morning responsibilities and to entrust to them an opportunity to create their ideal Shabbat morning service. Rabbis Janet and Shelly Marder created our New Emanuel Minyan, established the *matbeah tefillah*, and worked with several different cantorial soloists to create a style of music that was participatory as opposed to performance. On those *shabbatot* when I didn't have bar or bat mitzvah responsibilities, I was a congregant at the New Emanuel Minyan. For me it was a learning experience in the power of communal prayer.

In the early days the minyan met once a month, then twice. By the time Janet and Shelly moved on to other positions, I had been joined at Emanuel by my wonderful colleagues Rabbi Jonathan Aaron and Cantor Yonah Kliger. We continued where the Marders had left off. Now, with the New Emanuel Minyan meeting every Shabbat, Rabbi Aaron and I rotated leadership of the minyan and the bar mitzvah service in the sanctuary.

As I reflect on the question of transformation, the key was not only the excellence of the service created by the Marders, but, more importantly, the conscious decision to create a partnership between the clergy and the congregation. Once the minyan was meeting every Shabbat, we created a Worship Care Committee along the lines Larry Hoffman describes in his book *The Art of Public Prayer: Not for Clergy Only*. While it too has evolved over the years, the Worship Care effort is an ongoing process whereby congregants and clergy meet regularly to check in, talk about what is working and what isn't, and discuss the kinds of risks people feel ready to take. This effort led to the creation of our own prayer book, a labor of learning and love that involved about twenty congregants studying liturgy, reading poetry, and exploring how best to create a living siddur. The Worship Care Committee, understanding the importance of eating together in creating community, decided to have a kiddush lunch every week. Finally, the Worship Care effort led to the decision to hire a rabbinic intern whose job it would be to care for the minyan, to train the greeters, to act as gabbai, to send a weekly e-mail, to be present every week in a non-liturgical function in order to pay attention to who was there and who wasn't, to make sure new people are seated with regulars, and to nurture the sense of community. Our intern, Jill Zimmerman, noticed, for example, that people were refusing honors because they weren't sure what to do. So she raised this issue at a Worship Care meeting, where people then shared what they needed to learn in order to be able to own the worship experience. She then instituted a series of mini-classes, offered after lunch, taught by other minyan participants, on every-thing from when to bow during the recitation of the *Amida,* to what to do in a Torah service, to the history of prayer. This learning complemented the learning that goes on within the service. Instead of a formal *d'var Torah,* the tradition has evolved that one of the rabbis leads an interactive Torah discussion with prepared texts that are studied both in *chevruta* and in a larger group discussion. Rabbi Aaron and I try to coordinate our teachings so that, over the course of a year, we have demonstrated the various lenses through which one studies Torah.

The New Emanuel Minyan has become a subcommunity within the synagogue. It has spawned a *bikur holim* and bereavement effort and is often the setting where we try out new ideas. We now offer a minyan alternative at High Holy Day services, and our "high church" High Holiday services in the main sanctuary have been influenced by what goes on at the minyan. For example, we now have at least one group *aliyah* at every morning High Holiday service. We invite people who are wrestling with some issue that the Torah raises to come forward, explaining, for example, that if this is a year when they are longing to make a change or give birth to some-thing new, then the *aliyah* of God remembering Sarah is for them. To say that this breaks down the formality of a service with 1200 people is an understatement! We were able to take that risk because we already had a significant group of people who had experienced group *aliyot* in the minyan.

The success of the minyan enabled us to understand that compel-ling worship is important to Reform Jews and gave us the courage to be playful about other services. On different Friday nights we have different kinds of services, a monthly musical service called Shabbat Unplugged, a monthly service with an in-house band called *Shabbat B'yahad,* and a more intimate chapel service the other *shabbatot.* We are now instituting a Worship Care Committee for the chapel service and look forward to each service having its own worship care effort. This year, for the first time, because of the open-ness we have demonstrated about worship, some of our younger congregants (in their 20s and 30s) created their own Friday night alternative that meets once a month late on a Friday night. That service is totally lay led.

The New Emanuel Minyan is hardly new any more. But we are not changing the name. Because the minyan is a partnership between clergy and congregation, it is always changing and, therefore, always new. Sometimes innovations work; sometimes they don't. We talk about what we want to do, and we reflect on what we have done, together, congregation and clergy. It is an ongoing experiment, a good example of living Judaism.

The categories described in the article "Functional and Visionary Congregations" by Steven M. Cohen, Isa Aron, Lawrence Hoffman, and Ari Kelman are helpful as I reflect on the evolution of the minyan and the impact it has made at Temple Emanuel. The authors distinguish between functional and visionary synagogues. Functional synagogues are categorized by consumerist purpose, segmented understanding, passivity and excessive professional control, detachment, resistance to change, and non-reflective leadership. Visionary congregations, on the other hand, demonstrate sacred purpose, holistic ethos, participatory culture, meaningful engagement, innovative disposition, and reflective leadership.

In all honesty, I have to admit that Temple Emanuel is both at the same time. Much of what goes on is functional. Many people join in order that their children have a bar or bat mitzvah, but many, unfortunately, leave when it is over. Some join because they want to send their children to our day school, but leave after their children graduate. Still others join just to come for the High Holy Days or they view us as an insurance policy—they want to make sure someone who knows them will be there to officiate at their funerals.

On the other hand, there are subcommunities within the Temple that could be described as visionary. The New Emanuel Minyan is part of that vision—a sacred community with participatory culture, meaningful engagement, innovative disposition, and reflective leadership. And while those who participate in the minyan would speak about its "holistic ethos" (participants pray together, learn together, celebrate each other's *simhas* together, and comfort each other at times of loss), it is still a subcommunity within a larger congregation.

But, perhaps because of the New Emanuel Minyan, the congregation has changed and continues to change. The values reflected in the minyan support "visionary" work in the congregation. The experience of Torah study in the minyan has modeled one-on-one conversations between congregants, as well as other transformation projects, such as the social justice initiative with congregation-ally based community organizing that begins with one-on-one conversations. (It already had a base when we began and, in fact, it has drawn many of its leaders from that community.) Over the years, more and more board members have come to leadership positions through the minyan, and over the years more of our leaders have begun to come to the minyan. We continue to aspire to spend more time in reflection with our leaders.

We try our best to move from "functional" to "visionary," to transform our "consumers" into engaged members of a sacred community. We require, for example, that every bar or bat mitzvah family come at least once to the New Emanuel Minyan. Every year a few become regulars. We create an opportunity at bar and bat mitzvah family education programs for parents to discuss with each other their concerns for the future of their children in this privileged and stress-filled world. We send a daily Elul reflection by e-mail with a story by a congregant about a moment when the High Holy Days were particularly meaningful to him or her. This is a way to model part of what makes a sacred community: listening to each other's stories. Not everyone opens the e-mails, but many do and seem to be moved. We deliver *mishloah manot* to the doorstep of every congregant's home. Sometimes, when the congregants are home, they invite the one bringing the Purim basket to come in to visit. We've created an innovative teen philanthropy program in which our high school students serve as the board of directors of an endowment fund and, after researching organizations doing work they feel is important, determine how to give away the money. As a result, these teenagers have challenged the Temple's Endowment Board to reflect on whether Jewish values ought to influence how that endowment is invested. Congregants are talking with each other about things that matter, across generational lines, and more of our teenagers are staying connected to the temple. Slowly, slowly, we are coming closer to a congregation that matters in people's lives, a sacred community.

So perhaps one key to transformation is creating "visionary" communities and projects within "functional" synagogues and to remember that all synagogues are works in progress. While the work of transformation is far from over, at least one thing is clear: I do have a place to pray and a community that helps me remember what Emanuel means: "God is among us."

It's a beginning.

Restoring a Center City Congregation

Mitchell Chefitz

9:00 A.M., April 1, 2002. April Fools Day. I stand in the parking lot across the street from Temple Israel of Greater Miami, the old city cemetery behind me. Temple Israel is 80 years old, the cemetery, older. The silhouette of the buildings reminds me of my destroyer in the Gulf of Tonkin in 1966. That destroyer patrolled a five-mile course, back and forth, monitoring air traffic returning from strikes in North Vietnam. The temple floats on a sea of asphalt, but all I can think of is "dead in the water," my metaphor mixing as I contemplate the task ahead, wondering which task would prove more treacherous, ascending to the bridge of a destroyer at war or to the pulpit of a classical Reform congregation in decay.

Temple Israel of Greater Miami, once 1,800 households strong, 5,000 souls gathering for the Holy Days in the Convention Center, had a great rabbi, Joseph Narot, gone since 1980, and a great cantor, Jacob Bornstein, also gone. They left behind a fairy-tale beautiful sanctuary, a gaudily ornamented chapel, a ballroom auditorium, several meeting spaces, and 11,000 square feet of classrooms. Twenty years after the passing of Rabbi Narot, there remained fewer than 400 households, average age 75. The other 1,400 had moved on to either the suburbs or the next world.

The year before, when the temple had been unable to find a new rabbi, Chaim Stern, *z"l*, stepped from retirement into the breach but was taken within a few months, long enough to leave a positive impression, but no momentum. There had been no rabbi at the temple since shortly after the Holy Days.

MITCHELL CHEFITZ (NY75) is an author and scholar-in-residence at Temple Israel of Greater Miami, Florida. His latest work, *The Curse of Blessings*, a collection of spiritual stories, has been translated into German and Korean, and will soon appear in Mandarin.

Two weeks before, when I had accepted the position at Temple Israel, I had been summoned to the office of a friend and colleague, the Rosh Yeshivah of the Talmudic University.

"What are you doing?" he asked.

"No different from what I've been doing the last twenty years," I answered, "just in a different setting."

Since 1980 I had been experimenting with progressive outreach, the Havurah of South Florida, creating independent *havurot* in the vacuum of the Jewish community, the 85 percent who were unaffiliated with any Jewish institution. Havurah of South Florida met the religious and spiritual needs of over 300 souls, had over 200 programs and services each year, and attracted great spiritual teachers to intimate home venues.

But in the last years, after serious illness, my stamina had diminished. So I contemplated a career change. I began to write, travel, lecture, consult. The new career was bearing fruit. So why did I agree to interrupt that career to stand in the puddle of asphalt before a congregation that seemed in the last stages of steady decline?

The Mishnah *"B'makom sh'ein anashim, hishtadel l'hiyot ish"* was a part of it. There was no other rabbi readily available to guide the work. But also there was a curiosity. Could I reproduce an experiment in someone else's laboratory? Could I take the same approach to Jewish life that made the Havurah of South Florida a vital organization inside synagogue walls?

Temple Israel could not return to life as a conventional Reform congregation. It could not compete with successful suburban congregations for religious school and bar/bat mitzvah students. It had to create a program that would draw adults from great distances to spiritual sustenance they could not get elsewhere.

Who were these adults?

Some were progressive Jews who had gravitated to Chabad, Aish HaTorah, Young Israel, even the Kabbalah Centre, for lack of some other place to go where they might engage text and religious experience at an adult and profound level. This was our competition, to draw such Jews back to an institution that could provide this engagement and experience in a progressive and non-cultic environment and then reach out to those on the fringe of the Jewish world, to convince them there was something in the center city worth their time, resources, and energy.

That had been my work in the Havurah. Would it work within conventional walls?

My agreement with the temple was for five years, to create a bridge from what had been to what might be when 20,000 new condominiums would stand as close as two blocks away overlooking Biscayne Bay, bringing several thousand Jewish occupants into the neighborhood. My obligation was to bring enough vitality into the congregation to attract a good Reform rabbi to serve it long term. I hoped that after five years I could return to my writing career, to travel, teach, consult, and float on the cushion of Medicare.

I knew I couldn't do those five years alone.

There were resources within the temple, a small, dedicated group of older members still with the energy and will to continue, and a small, dedicated group of younger members, mostly children of members, but some newcomers eager to see the temple return to health. Among the newcomers were members of Ruach, the GLBT havurah that had been welcomed inside the synagogue walls.

Professional staff included a core of dedicated workers in the administrative offices, and Dr. Alan Mason, the director of music, who had within him the liturgical history of the temple and talent beyond measure at the piano.

There was also a recent immigrant form Buenos Aries who had grown up under the tutelage of Marshall Meyer, z"l. She was the backup to the cantorial soloist. She was a tango singer, a cabaret performer, a recording artist who could sing in Spanish, Hebrew, English, and Ladino. Karina Zilberman was not a conventional cantor or soloist, but perfect for what I had in mind. Before I accepted the position at Temple Israel, we met and decided this was an endeavor we would attempt together.

So we began.

Five years later we had nearly 500 households, average age 54. The increase consisted of younger adults, mostly empty-nesters, intent upon serious Jewish learning and experience. Toward the end of those five years the congregation began its search for a new rabbi and had over twenty applicants.

What did we do? We set a goal across the Jewish horizon, maintained focus throughout the five years, and drew all temple activity in that direction. The goal was to create an educated and responsible Jewish laity capable of extending progressive Judaism beyond its current frontier.

The basic principles:

- Judaism is for adults. If we make Jewish adults, the Jewish adults will make Jewish children.
- Adult Jews are smart. Most all have college degrees, if not graduate degrees. Therefore address congregants at the graduate, not the entry, level.
- Get out of the way. (*Tzimtzum.*) Leave room for the congregants to reach and grow. The congregation belongs to them, not to the clergy.

There's nothing new there. Larry Kushner expressed it well in his "Tent Peg" article, first published in *New Traditions*, the journal of the National Havurah Committee in 1984, now posted on the URJ website.

We began by advertising a series of four Holy Day workshops, promising a profound, spiritual experience. Attendance increased with each workshop as word spread that we could deliver on our promise. Alan and Karina taught the musical experience. I taught the most difficult texts I could find concerning *tefillah* and *teshuvah*. Why did I choose difficult texts, and why do I continue to do so?

- If I teach what is difficult and admit I don't understand the text completely, I cannot fail. I invite creative interaction.
- If I choose something easy and the students don't grasp it, they feel foolish. On the other hand, if I choose something difficult and the students grasp even a little, it's a great accomplishment. Likely they will grasp more than a little and succeed beyond all expectations.
- If I repeat material the students heard back in religious school yet one more time, they won't return to hear the same thing again. Every experience has to be new and challenging.

The result of the workshops was a critical mass expecting a profound experience at the Holy Day services. It wasn't Alan, Karina, and I who provided the experience for them. It was the members who took risks in participating that enabled them to achieve it. The expectation of something spontaneous held the new participants on the edge of their seats. The service was always the message, not the sermon. Prayer was prayer, not pageantry or instruction. The congregation sensed quickly the change in tone and intensity.

How did the older members react? At first they chafed at what was new, but, on the other hand, they turned around to see the sanctuary full. I listened to their complaints patiently until we became friends.

Not everything we tried worked. The very nature of risk invites occasional failure. But it was readily acknowledged that risks had to be taken. So the failures were tolerated while the successes far outweighed the setbacks.

The Havurah of South Florida never had a religious school. There was only family education. It took some years to blend such intergenerational education into the small religious school of Temple Israel, but it became the accepted norm in the last few of the five years.

Regular learning developed on Shabbat morning, but not a regular service. Thirty, forty, or more gathered around tables to learn text—difficult text, of course. The learning was preceded by blessings, concluded with meditation and prayer, but it never became a conventional service. A few families that were regular participants at those tables chose to celebrate a bar or bat mitzvah there, but most families chose to create a unique service in the sanctuary. With only eight to ten such celebrations a year, it was easy to do.

A tradition in the Havurah was for each bar or bat mitzvah to take the Torah scroll home the week before his or her service. The Havurah had no building. The Torah scroll moved regularly from home to home. I continued this tradition at Temple Israel to good effect, and then took it one step further.

Within a few years Temple Israel had become a religious institution, its focus on divine service, whether through Torah, prayer, or social justice. Fund-raising at Temple Israel had followed conventional paths: honoring a person at a dinner, casino night, raffles. If there was a single moment that indicated a shift, it was at a fund-raising committee meeting in the third year. The committee had run out of people to honor. It was considering a golf tournament, among other devices. Then, the executive director, Amy Mallor, proposed restoring a Torah scroll that had fallen into disrepair. This classical Reform congregation had never done such a thing. The argument was subtle and persuasive. "We have become a community focused on divine service. What most moves us in that direction? A golf tournament? A casino night? A raffle? Or the restoration of a Torah scroll?" Writing or restoring a Torah scroll is a time-honored institution in a great many congregations, but it was new to this one.

I added an additional innovation. Since this was Florida, the land of the timeshare, we would invite members to underwrite a *parashah*, and that would become a timeshare. The week of the *parashah* the family could welcome the restored Torah into its home, with an appropriate program or celebration. The restoration of that Torah scroll raised four times the amount of funds expected. It also raised consciousness concerning Torah from household to household.

My five years are over. Constructing that bridge from what had been to what could be was a great adventure. The 20,000 condominium units were also constructed, but, because of the economy, they stand empty. So the bridge is still very much in the air, not yet grounded on the other side of the chasm.

The momentum of learning continues. We have a new senior rabbi on board. The temple facility is in good repair. Will all remain in good repair long enough for the economy to turn around, for the neighborhood to develop, for Jews to move in? It will be a difficult task. But, better difficult than easy, for if we succeed even a little, the accomplishment will be great.

A Do-It-Yourself Shul

Lydia Kukoff

The Chatham Synagogue Netivot Torah (TCS) needed a new mantle for its Torah…and therein lies a tale of our do-it-yourself shul.

It starts with wool from local sheep, owned by (non-Jewish) women who spun the wool at the Chatham County Fair. A sign nearby explained that this wool was for a Torah mantle for TCS (lots of explaining there). These women, who had never been in a synagogue and had never seen a Torah, up and decided to donate their wool. The inspiration for the design emerged from our Shabbat morning Torah discussions, specifically, the description of the colors in the *mishkan*. The design itself was created by one of our members, an architect, in collaboration with the Building Committee. Over many months the dyeing and the weaving was done by a local (non-Jewish) woman and the fabrication by a local (non-Jewish) man. The beautiful mantle, displayed at the following year's fair, was a first for everyone concerned and a real *sheheheyanu* for our shul. TCS, located in Chatham, New York, a small, rural town equidistant to Albany and the Berkshires, looks to our membership and our community for what we need.

Established in 1999 as the Synagogue at Malden Bridge, TCS began with a dozen households that set out to create a congregation in the northern end of Columbia County, an agricultural area that, over the years, has become a magnet for transplants, retirees, and second-home owners, largely from the New York City metropolitan area. While a long-standing congregation existed in Hudson, the county seat, no synagogue had ever served the needs of the northern end of the county, where the most significant demographic changes were occurring.

LYDIA KUKOFF (MAJS LA78) is immediate past president of The Chatham Synagogue and was the first director of the UAHC-CCAR Commission on Reform Jewish Outreach.

From our beginnings we knew we would be dealing with a population with disparate needs. We chose to model ourselves after Abraham and Sarah's tent, with all four sides open, welcoming any and all who sought to enter. Our hope was—and is—that we can create a *mishkan*, a (lower case "s") sanctuary for all Jews in our area who choose to enter. TCS believes in serious religious practice, and we have given great thought to the ways in which we balance the traditional and the innovative in our services and programs. Many members who have had only the most rudimentary experience with Judaism find themselves becoming regular Shabbat morning shulgoers, knowing that they have found a place where they can progress on their spiritual journey at their own pace, with the support of others who are on a similar path.

We chose a transdenominational, pluralistic approach to Jewish life, not just as a reflection of the diverse backgrounds of our members, but as a reflection of our values. By choosing not to belong to a denomination we are forced to live in the questions. We have to arrive at our own policies as a community. This is not always easy, but it is always educational and engaging. Together, as a community, we have grappled with difficult issues—*kashrut*, matrilineal-patrilineal—and found a way to arrive at consensus. Learning how to deal with complicated issues together as a community—with tradition as our guide, but not our governor—how to agree, to disagree, and agree to disagree, to listen to each other with respect, to come to understand that our disagreements are *l'shem shamayim*, has strengthened the culture of our community.

We chose to be a member-led, volunteer congregation. We believe that this decision leads to a greater sense of ownership. We really could not exist without our members. They create the programs and materials, run the weekly services, oversee our building. We rely on our human resources, a constantly expanding, rich pool of interesting, talented, energetic people. Each person matters, and each person knows it. Each person has a gift to give. As new people enter our community, we ask for their help.

Early on, we created a mission statement:

> The Chatham Synagogue Netivot Torah has chosen to be an unaffiliated congregation that serves a diverse population of Jews in our region. As a community, we carry on the tradition of simplicity and modesty in keeping with rural synagogues of the past. At the same time, we have a contemporary view of that tradition.

We believe in equality at the bimah, in a vital and searching study of Torah, in maintaining the tradition of Hebrew as part of the service, and in the ability of each individual to find his or her own meaningful relationship with Jewish culture, heritage and religion. We believe the synagogue should play a central role in that pursuit, that a Jewish community is a blessing and that being part of one is a mitzvah.

As a congregation, we aspire to:

- provide a home for egalitarian worship in accordance with the traditions of Judaism
- encourage and deepen a love and knowledge of Jewish practices, principles, and culture among our members
- be a source of education for our members, future generations, and the larger Jewish community
- play an active role in the larger community, both in terms of providing a Jewish presence and by promoting social justice

Recognizing that Jews understand their sense of Jewishness in diverse ways, we decided to create different portals though which they might enter.

Worship

We offer services every Shabbat and on holidays. Rabbi Or Rose, our visiting scholar, leads services and conducts workshops once a month and has been an invaluable resource. High Holy Day services, led by Rabbi Rose with participation by members, are open to all without charge.

There were many challenges at the beginning. One of the first challenges was to create a service that would be inclusive, respecting the diversity of Jewish knowledge, experience, and observance in our community. Our members came from different synagogues —or no synagogues. Some wanted more Hebrew, some less. Some wanted more singing, some less. Most had never heard of Carlebach, much less his melodies. While the more participatory service we were developing was welcome to most, choosing a *siddur* was another early challenge. With our community's needs in mind, the Ritual Committee examined many *siddurim* and recommended one that reflected a traditional service and included Hebrew, English, and transliterations, as well as beautiful readings. Our *tefilah* has evolved and has come to include spirited davening and an ever-expanding repertoire of *niggunim*, led by a cadre of members, most of whom have never before led services. We have developed engaging services that strike a balance between tradition and innovation and that are satisfying. They continue to evolve. The Ritual Committee, working with one of our members, a graphic artist, has just produced and distributed to members a beautifully designed booklet containing additional transliterations and more information about the prayers. It is accompanied by a CD of prayers and *niggunim,* sung by a member.

A highlight of the service is TCS's distinctive treatment of the weekly *parasha.* Instead of chanting in Hebrew, we have a member-led, roundtable reading of the entire portion in English. Participants, new and veteran, join in a lively exchange that can touch on sources from Rashi to Jung to Cynthia Ozick to Mel Brooks, with a dash of ancient history and personal experience thrown in. Our members, who run the gamut from the Jewishly knowledgeable to the cautiously curious, have come to take great pleasure in wrestling with text.

Adult Study

In addition to the weekly discussion of the *parasha,* the monthly workshops led by Rabbi Rose are a focal point of study at TCS. A topic for the year is chosen: last year, "Jewish Views of God," using Gillman's book; this year, "Healing a Broken World: Personal and Communal Transformation," using Dorff's book. In addition, we have held one-day Hebrew marathons, beginning Talmud classes, and discussion groups, all member-led.

Culture

Our area is rich in cultural offerings and we number among our members writers, actors, composers, and architects. Early in our existence, we acquired a giant-screen television set, enabling us to develop our microcinema, which features films of Jewish interest regularly throughout the year. (We recently held a Kafka mini-series.) Since these films are followed by a discussion and refreshments, they have become valuable opportunities to create community. Coming to a film at the microcinema was the first time many of our members set foot in the shul. We also offer different series, such as "Conversation Pieces," which has featured salon-setting presentations of the work of members and friends, and the Jewish Discussion Group, as well as book discussion groups.

Families

Although the synagogue's demography tends to be older, TCS has created an environment that feels right for families and their young children. We have a small Hebrew school and children-led *kabbalat* Shabbat services. Families gather for Shabbat and holiday potlucks. Children participate in mitzvah projects, such as baking for a Salvation Army shelter or gleaning in the fields at harvest time for the community food pantry.

Tikkun Olam

TCS participates in community interfaith efforts, such as the community food pantry and School Supply Weekend. Before holidays, we visit Jewish residents in nursing homes. We hope this year's study with Rabbi Rose will aid us in expanding our social action agenda.

Community

From the beginning, we understood that synagogue and community are inseparable. Community is created every day, whether through frequent potlucks in the shul or in members' homes, the warm welcome given everyone who walks in the door, being present for each other in times of joy or need, or the myriad ways caring is expressed in our interactions with each other. Many of TCS's members are new to the area (i.e., have relocated within the last five years) and arrive without significant local connections. The synagogue often becomes the keystone of their social structure. TCS's open tent philosophy is not just spoken; it is lived. Elders co-exist with the young, straight with gay, affluent with struggling, knowledgeable with novice, all committed to this undertaking that has egalitarianism and simplicity at its core.

Our first decision had been to focus on building a community, and not to focus on a building. We were very fortunate, for our first five years, to be housed in a Methodist church that charged us minimal rent. Our relationship with the church provided a wonderful opportunity to create a sense of grass-roots, interfaith commonality that has remained such an important element in the life of TCS. In fact, TCS has come to be a heretofore unseen Jewish presence in the larger Chatham community.

Our Building

In 2005, we were able to secure our own permanent home. The former Chatham Town Hall, which started out life as a turn-of-the-century schoolhouse, was put up for sale and, in a leap of faith (the shul had never done any fund-raising), we bought it. Purchase price, renovation and furnishings totaled $330,000. Our building was entirely funded by member donations, fund-raising events, and no- or low- interest loans from members. We relied on the skills and talents of members. The re-design was developed and overseen by a member who is an architect. As with all our materials, all solicitations to members and the community were written, designed, and printed at no cost to the synagogue. Fund-raising events, such as a lecture on Chagall by his granddaughter (a TCS member), a staged reading of a published play written by a member, directed by another, tag sales coordinated by members and featuring member donations, and a silent auction with goods and services provided by members enabled us to pay back the last of our loans this past spring. The synagogue has been able to accomplish this feat with all giving being anonymous and without "naming opportunities" or a building fund, which we believe run counter to the egalitarian ethos that is essential to a volunteer-driven organization.

Our building is ideal for our needs. It is centrally located and its facilities are adequate for the size of our congregation, which now numbers almost one hundred households. This solid, unpretentious building also reflects the shul's esthetic of simplicity and modesty, which recalls our area's Shaker tradition and its history as the site of a Baron de Hirsch Jewish agricultural settlement in the early 1900s. In its permanent home, TCS has eschewed any ornate decoration—no stained glass, no wall hangings, nothing but a simple ledge, hand-made by a member, upon which sits a simple ark, hand-made by a member. The sanctuary is decorated only by some simple graphics, such as the inscription *"…l'hitatef ba'tzitzit"* above the *talitot* that hang on dowels on the wall. Members and visitors often comment on the serenity of this sacred space and how that serenity helps facilitate their spiritual explorations.

We are always thinking about the future. We have completed a planning process that will guide us over the next several years and are revising our by-laws. We have just developed a Jewish cemetery, designed by another of our architect members. We hope to create a *hevra kadishah*. Our programming grows apace.

As we approach our tenth anniversary, we can see all that we have accomplished. We have grown organically and we have managed our growth, maintaining the healthy culture that we developed. We refer often to our mission statement, making sure that everything we do is mission-consistent. Our simple little country shul is not so simple. We have grown, becoming a more complex organism, and that brings challenges:

Decision-making, transparency, communication

We have a seventeen-member Board, numerous very active committees, and many programs and projects occurring or in development. A significant number of our members divide their time between city and country. We have tried to improve communication by having Board members receive minutes of each committee meeting. We have a weekly e-mail update, a quarterly newsletter and an expanded website. In addition, each member receives a looseleaf handbook containing the history of TCS, our mission statement, driving directions, a membership list, and a list of all committees, including their mission and their chairpersons.

Leadership development

Our model is quite labor intensive and can easily lead to burnout. We have taken care not to create an inverted triangle wherein proliferating programs are the responsibility of the same few people. Each program has a point person. We bring new people into the system through our committees. Potential leaders then can advance to the Board. The sole criteria for running for the Board are demonstrated leadership ability and willingness to take on even more responsibility. We have Board members who are founders and Board members who joined the synagogue within the last couple of years. Committee chairs change and we have term limits for Board members.

We acquired our building during the week of *Parashat Terumah*. Many of us were moved to tears as we read *"ve'asu li mikdash ve'shachanti be'tocham"*—"Let them build me a sanctuary and I will dwell among them," the words (in Hebrew and English) that now greet members and guests as they enter our shul. These words remind us that what we have created is really something very elemental: a community of people who care about each other, who care about the larger community, who have had the experience of creating sacred space in whatever environment they happen to be occupying, who think locally, simply, and modestly, and who work very hard at what they do—a simple prescription, but, in fact, perhaps a radical approach to the question of synagogue-building in these complicated times.

Reflections

Our population

We are an exurban community. Jews who are moving here, either full- or part-time, are generally empty-nesters. Unless the local economy changes significantly to make it attractive to young Jewish families, our growth will continue to be with this demographic. These empty-nesters bring great energy, life experience, and professional skills, as well as time to devote to our enterprise. We anticipate that we will remain at about 100 households for the foreseeable future, possibly eventually growing to a maximum of 125.

Our strengths

From the beginning, we had a clear vision, which we were able to communicate: to be like Abraham and Sarah's tent, open on all four sides, inclusive; to provide different portals through which Jews could enter and find\create community; to incorporate the values of modesty, simplicity, egalitarianism; to empower Jews to own Judaism and be active in claiming or reclaiming it.

The vision was compelling, but the challenge was to make it real. We translated our vision into programs. As important, we worked to create a healthy culture. This was perhaps our most difficult early challenge, but also possibly the most critical. We had to learn how to have respectful communal discourse, to create boundaries, to deal with problematic individuals or situations (especially in such a small community). We had to learn to be a community. Everyone doesn't have to be everyone else's (best) friend, but we have to function with a sense of *derech eretz*.

People join the synagogue for different reasons. Some choose to be more involved and some, less so. There is no judgment. Managing the human dynamic was a major factor in creating the positive energy that is so much a part of who we are to this day. With our demographic, there is no external reason for people to join a synagogue. There is a great deal for people to do in the larger community—concerts, lectures, art, volunteer opportunities. They join the synagogue because of the spirit, the energy, the people, and they stay and become involved because of what they subsequently discover as Jews and as members of a Jewish community. We have had remarkably little attrition.

Decision-making without a rabbi or movement affiliation has become an opportunity to educate ourselves as a community and to explore some of our most deeply held feelings.

Since our early days, a handful of people meeting in the back room of the Methodist church, we have managed change and growth by remaining mission-consistent and trusting ourselves. There was some anxiety about the move from the small room to our own building. Would something be lost? Would our "simple country shul" become something else? Who we were moved with us, and having our own building enabled us to flourish. Beneath our "haimishness" we are very highly organized but we don't feel like an organization. Although we are all volunteers, there is a great sense of accountability. Programs emanate from members and friends and are high quality and mission-consistent. One of our members, a graphic artist, created our graphic look and creates and produces our materials. Press releases and other publicity are done by another member, a PR professional.

Jewish Community Project

Darren Levine

At the Jewish Community Project (JCP Downtown) we are experimenting with a new community model in Lower Manhattan. Not a synagogue, not a JCC, not a Hillel, we are a project—organic and evolving.

JCP was started six years ago by a handful of young families looking for Jewish community following 9/11. One neighbor invited another, and then another another, until together they had created a children's Purim party in 2002 that turned out to be the inspiration of JCP Downtown. Six years later, JCP has over 700 families connected to the Project, a preschool of 100 children, daily after-school programs for elementary ages, Shabbat experiences, and holiday programs, ten full-time staff members, and approximately thirty teachers and faculty. Our 10,000 sq. feet has classroom space, a cafe, a rock-climbing wall, and is in the center of a fast-growing residential neighborhood in Lower Manhattan called Tribeca.

To the outside eye, JCP might look like many other urban congregations that have nursery schools, social action programs, and Shabbat and holiday gatherings. Yet, beneath the surface, there are a few features that make JCP unique: its members' diversity of background and its leaders' self-conscious determination to set aside old models of Jewish organizations to create our own purposeful, meaningful, and accessible way of creating Jewish community today.

JCP is made up almost exclusively of families with children who have chosen to build their lives in downtown Manhattan. Most JCP participants have strong Jewish identities and are hungry for Jewish community, for deepening friendships with their Jewish neighbors, and for giving their children an authentic sense of Jewish tradition.

DARREN LEVINE, D.Min (NY 03) is Executive Director of the Jewish Community Project (JCP Downtown) in Lower Manhattan.

Their backgrounds are Orthodox, Conservative, Reform, non-practicing, secular, or interfaith. Some are Jewish day school graduates, others grew up connected to synagogues or JCCs or neither. For many raised in other faiths or none, JCP is their first Jewish experience. They are every race and sexual preference. This diversity is in the air they breathe and the style community we are creating reflects its value as core to the mission.

In another era, the so-called "shul with the pool" model reflected the need of Jews as they moved to the suburbs to create all-encompassing communities for themselves. Today in downtown Manhattan, I often use the image of a pool to describe JCP's philosophy of how people enter Jewish life today. Like swimmers in a pool, some like the shallow end, others the deep end. Some jump right in and make a big splash, little splash, or no splash. Some start in the shallow end and swim to the deep end. Some participants love the water, others find it intimidating, and yet others tolerate it multiple access, multiple entry points, all valued as equal. And for me, depending on the moment, I play the role of life-guard, observing the volunteers and staff create programs; other times I am the coach, leading and inspiring; and, sometimes I am the general manager, directing and barking.

To create this type of inclusive and multi-entry environment at JCP, we focus on three areas: empowering volunteer leadership, creating diverse and pluralistic programming options, and developing a diverse professional staff and clergy that values and appreciates many expressions of Jewish life.

Empowering Volunteer Leadership

At JCP we are blessed with many participants ready and able to take on leadership positions, some because of leadership training in movement camps and youth groups, and many because of their personal orientation as urban pioneers downtown. Participation as a leader is an expectation that is built into the DNA at JCP. As we've grown rapidly, greater attention has been given to developing structures to support shared leadership. A Community Involvement Team made up of staff and volunteers has as its mandate the charge to pursue each community member to encourage active engagement in one or more aspects of the organization that interests him or her. Volunteer leaders create, design, and implement many programs and as a result, they take a genuine ownership of the organization. It also diffuses a core power structure because many contribute to decision-making.

Diverse and Pluralistic Program

Like the majority of synagogues from which JCP members come, the synagogue where I grew up had one Shabbat service, one educational system, one rabbi, one bar/bat mitzvah service. If you wanted another, you looked for another synagogue.

At JCP, we are attempting to create a program whose diversity matches that of the community. Some families send their young children to our preschool that meets five days per week, while others attend weekly Jewish music, art, and story-time classes. The "religious school" has two or three tracks: from a monthly intensive to weekly sessions, to our Kesher program that meets twice per week for six hours and occasional weekends. This multi-access model appreciates and respects the range of *hashkafah*, Jewish and secular, of today's Jewish community.

What these multiple pathways create in terms of the overall community are concentric circles of smaller networks that intersect one another in a non-denominational based setting. We're trying many access points, which will put freedom into the hands of the participant. It's the internet model of social networking applied to a living, organic, and localized community organization.

Pluralistic Minded Staff and Clergy

These programmatic goals and the continual regeneration and deepening of the overall volunteer structure demand a particular staffing model, which has grown as JCP Downtown has grown. Each staff member has a genuine appreciation for the complex nuances that shape Jewish identity and our staff comes from varied backgrounds. I am a product of the Reform Movement and an HUC-JIR-trained rabbi, our director of Jewish life served a Conservative leaning congregation for seven years, and our Early Childhood director attended Yeshiva through high school, as did the current chair of the board. A YU-trained Orthodox rabbi hosts monthly Shabbat dinners for singles and couples without children. For all of us, it's an experiment in breaking down divisions and finding common Jewish ground.

The final element that ties it all together is how we deploy our staff. In the best cases, program professionals are working with constituencies that reflect their own personal demographic. The rabbi who is cultivating the 20s and 30s singles and young couples is himself a 30-something single rabbi. The director of the Early Childhood Center is herself a parent of a toddler. Wherever possible, we are finding the most receptivity among the volunteers and participants when the community can speak of the staff members as "one of us."

My own observation is that these young Jewish families are looking locally for one place to call their Jewish home and they are ready to step up with energy and passion to a project that matches their vision. Multiple affiliations between JCC's, synagogues, schools, etc., spread them too thin in a busy world. A pluralistic model like JCP draws on participant strengths to create common ground without regard to movement labels. Strong volunteer leadership and programmatic responsibility give members a genuine feeling of ownership as they expand their network of friendships and human connections. And finally, JCP staff members, who understand the access points at all depths of the pool, often bring complementary skills to help Jews dip their toe, wade, jump, dive, and even plunge. Combine all this with some Torah, *ruach*, and smoked fish, and the result is a creative new "project" of meaningful Jewish community.

HUC-JIR and the Creation of Visionary Jewish Leadership

Aaron D. Panken

Now more than ever, American Jewish seminaries educate under novel conditions. These conditions include an array of changes in the formation of our student body, the makeup of our faculty, and our curriculum; they also include numerous pressing questions that have arisen of late in the communal settings in which our students and graduates work. In response, Hebrew Union College-Jewish Institute of Religion has undergone its own process of transformation in an effort to shape specific answers to these formidable new questions and challenges.

First, a few words about the changed context. Our student body now includes an ever more diverse array of individuals who enter seminary doors with wildly varied notions of professional life shaped by their prior communal experiences. This diversity of student background is an increasingly important factor in the creation of Jewish professionals who understand what it means to build visionary institutions and transform established ones. While many of our students still come from those who "rise through the ranks" in the Reform movement via religious school, camp, NFTY and college programs, it is now the rule rather than the exception that our students arrive after a wider, more pluralistic assortment of prior Jewish experiences.

Some turn up fresh from the university, still reeling from the process of becoming a Jewish adult in a variegated Hillel setting that has exposed them to viewpoints that Sunday school never prepared them for; others arrive after long, successful careers with copious life

AARON D. PANKEN, Ph.D., (NY91) is Vice President for Strategic Initiatives, HUC-JIR.

experience in multiple Jewish communities. Many have attended or led local synagogues and *minyanim* of all stripes, experimenting with different sorts of Jewish worship regardless of stated affiliation or disaffiliation. Most have partaken of a wide range of in-depth study experiences—in North America or in Israel; in Hebrew or in English; with academic credit or without; and in Reform and non-Reform settings (from Humanistic Judaism and JCCs to Chabad, Aish HaTorah, and beyond). They bring to their student lives the particular viewpoints and questions that arose in those experiences. Nowadays, a majority of students at HUC-JIR have experimented with Jewish life outside the Reform movement at some point, but have ultimately returned to it because they share its values and commitments to pluralism, egalitarianism, inclusiveness, and social justice.

While in seminary, these students interact with a faculty that is also far more diverse and multi-faceted than ever before. In past decades, faculty members were often men drawn from a pool of loyal rabbinical graduates encouraged to continue at their *alma mater* for the Ph.D. They were infused with a sense of commitment to both the movement's priorities and the values of academic objectivity. Presently, younger seminary faculty members of both genders now train at top universities and learn their disciplines under advisors whose academic approach would eschew even the slightest hint of religious subjectivity. In their personal lives, the religious commitments of current faculty also vary greatly—there are faculty members who participate and lead active Jewish lives in every Jewish denomination, just as there are those whose only connection to Judaism is through academic channels. This particular combination of diversity of students and faculty enables a rich and wide-ranging conversation on the future of Judaism that extends farther afield than what existed in the past.

During their education at HUC-JIR, students question the norms they encounter with gusto, often in more than one direction at a time. At times, students profess a desire for what might be considered a more "traditional" stance: they wonder aloud if the movement focuses enough on practice and ritual, on study and the preparation of knowledgeable Jews. They experiment with *kashrut*, *Shabbat*, and ritual garb and infuse into worship words long removed from the Reform liturgical canon. They inquire as to whether Reform movement decisions such as patrilineal descent or the definition of the role of the non-Jewish spouse in congregations truly reflect appropriate understanding of our inherited tradition. They hunger for methods of study one might find in a traditional *yeshiva*—the *beit Midrash,* the learned *derashah,* and constant *hevruta* with fellow students—and they try to hold themselves to ever higher standards in their own text skills, intellectual development, and ability to access and transmit the Jewish tradition.

Simultaneously, and perhaps paradoxically, these same students strenuously question other boundaries set by our movement. They grapple with the dilemma of intermarriage and come to many discrete personal conclusions, some in agreement with stated movement policy, others in principled opposition. They ponder positive outreach efforts, yet ask if our movement does enough in-reach and education for our core community, let alone for those on the periphery. They regularly redefine the "standardized" roles of rabbis, cantors, and educators, slipping effortlessly (and admirably) among the leadership tasks in *tefillah,* teaching, and leading music. They frequently question the meaning of current modes of "synagogue membership" and are on the lookout for new models for vibrant congregational life. And while the vast majority will continue on into Reform congregational life after graduation, they will also look broadly, far beyond the Reform movement, for organizations, activities, and causes they consider sacred, into which they can pour their time and energy.

Beyond our doors, congregational life has also changed significantly and the seminary community clearly feels that. Where fifteen to twenty years ago the "buzz" during senior placement centered on whether a congregation would accept a female rabbi, whether a graduate should speak openly of his or her homosexuality, or whether a senior rabbi or ritual committee permitted the wearing of a *talit* or *kippah* on the *bimah,* today these questions have been (largely, albeit certainly not always perfectly) answered. New questions have emerged that have captured the attention of search committees looking to hire seminary graduates: Do they think outside the box? Are they willing to take risks in their leadership? Will they help come up with new models of education, outreach, and inclusion that can reach those who remain distant? Do they lead inspiring prayer that touches the hearts and minds of their *kahal?* Can they counsel those in need? And, my personal favorite: how good are they at "managing change"?

The world, then, has changed significantly for seminaries and for our students. Our alumni are well aware of and already quite expert at handling change and transformation—after learning "in the trenches," they do it every day. But such a different context also requires an altered approach to the initial education of clergy, and the College-Institute has worked hard at crafting new approaches over the past decade. We have attempted, where possible, not simply to be shaped by contextual change, but to shape it actively through our actions and contributions. (Think of the many experts on synagogue studies and education who work directly on improving congregations from their base at HUC-JIR: Lawrence Hoffman, Isa Aron, Stephen Cohen, Sam Joseph, Jo Kay, and so on, and you get the idea.) I will dedicate the rest of this essay to describing just a few of the many recent transformations HUC-JIR has made in reshaping curricular and extracurricular approaches to help shape a constructive response to this new context.

Curriculum, Raising Standards, and Assessment

One key area of growth in HUC-JIR's education of clergy can be found in the recent development of the rabbinical school's new core curriculum. This new curriculum was the first element of an overall review of curriculum that is now continuing in other programs around the institution. Designed by a committee of faculty from all campuses, the review of the rabbinical school curriculum had five explicit goals, as recounted by Provost Norman J. Cohen:

1. Integrate the Judaica knowledge, professional-skills learning, and religious growth of our rabbinical students;
2. Better integrate the First Year Program in Jerusalem into the broader curriculum;
3. Enhance the academic growth of our students by raising matriculation requirements in both Hebrew and basic Judaic knowledge;
4. Create a holistic learning experience; and
5. Build students' professional skills in counseling, education, leadership training, and synagogue change by establishing new requirements for mentored in-field experiences.

The similarity of this list of goals to the qualities that Aron *et al.* utilize to define a visionary congregation is readily apparent. Focus upon sacred purpose and sacred community combines with creating a holistic ethos when we integrate Judaic knowledge, professional skills, and religious growth (goals 1, 2, 4). Reflective leadership and a participatory culture emerge in the mentored in-field experiences that build students' professional skills in key areas of congregational vision (the counseling, education, leadership, and change management skills of goal 5).

The curricular review added one more element (goal 3) above and beyond those present in the visionary congregation typology—the building of a solid base of knowledge in advance of study, which allows ever higher standards for both entering and graduating students (raising educational standards, I would hope, is a prime candidate for version 2.0 of Aron *et al.*'s visionary list). This reflects a truism inherent in every literary description of rabbinical leadership from the first rabbis until now: while holistic ethos, reflective leadership and sacred purpose are all necessary, they are not by themselves sufficient to make one an effective rabbi if one knows little about Jewish tradition. Parenthetically, I would argue the same principle holds true for laity. Effective lay leaders also need to achieve a high level of Jewish knowledge, or their decisions, commitments, and values may not reflect their religious tradition appropriately.

Raising standards has already resulted in enhanced admissions criteria (higher Hebrew levels, better knowledge of basic Judaica, more experience in the Jewish community before admission, etc.), and the establishment of a detailed evaluation matrix for all levels of rabbinical students during their career at HUC-JIR. A national assessment committee, with the help of the entire faculty, carefully crafted protocols for ongoing formative assessment, and is now implementing focused summative assessment as well. Formative assessment follows students along their path through the College-Institute, ensuring that mentors assist with their formation by constantly promoting reflection and providing feedback as they grow. Summative assessment, in contrast, assesses students at special points of summation—after their first year in Israel, at the completion of the M.A.H.L., before ordination, etc. These dual assessments help students retain and integrate academic material across the required areas of the program, and create opportunities to reflect upon their learning and how it has shaped them as Jews and as future professionals.

In the professional learning areas, we have also witnessed immense growth. Our curriculum now couples theory with practice and supervision in a way that transcends prior approaches.

Students now participate in required classes in education and pastoral care that are accompanied by mentored field experiences that help them put theory into practice. As they have for decades, students benefit from pulpit placements in small congregations and internships in larger settings, where they learn to thrive as Jewish professionals. Now, however, they also benefit from the experiences of Clinical Pastoral Education internships, placements where they work with mental health professionals on bereavement, divorce or teen issues, camp and youth group work, educational internships, and other vocational opportunities where they are supervised by our own in-house experts as well as by seasoned field supervisors. The unique combination of internal academic supervision coupled with a team of expert external clinical practitioners makes these experiences tremendously fulfilling and fosters enormous professional growth for our students. It also provides contact with model alumni/ae who are constantly engaged in their own growth and learning while they help build the next generation of Jewish leadership.

Leadership, Outreach, and Social Justice

Over the past decade, HUC-JIR students have benefited from a number of programs that have created transformational leadership-training opportunities in diverse fields of study. These opportunities have helped students gain immeasurably in the areas of leadership training, outreach, and social justice. The programs utilize informal co-curricular learning settings, in which students have the opportunity to learn more about effective modes of education that transcend the classroom. Funded by the generosity and supported by the vision of a number of leading foundations and individuals, these projects have added considerably to the skills and vision of our students. HUC-JIR's close, intensive relationship with multiple funders also models for students the sort of enriching, creative partnerships they, too, will need to form with future supporters to enact their own vision in congregational life. I will enumerate just a few of these programs below.

The Charles and Lynn Schusterman Family Foundation recently funded a Program Chair in Leadership and Outreach, an initiative that has promoted numerous opportunities for learning leadership skills, social justice strategies, and discussing outreach techniques. Along with the recently established Rabbi Jerome Davidson Chair in Social Responsibility, this gift has prompted the development of a series of courses integrated into the professional development program on all campuses. These courses help rabbinical students develop skills and ideas in critical areas of leadership in social justice and help our students understand how to promote commitment and responsibility and bring to life the values encapsulated in Jewish texts and traditions. Through in-class experiences, internships, reflective retreat settings, and mentored, on-site fieldwork in successful congregations, the Schusterman program also focuses on outreach and developing intelligent, compassionate responses to interfaith families and couples considering intermarriage. These activities ensure that our students are far better prepared than their predecessors for the growing complexities they will face in the congregations and Jewish organizations they serve.

Visionary congregations, more than ever before, must carefully consider how they structure welcoming, open-learning opportunities for both Jews and non-Jews. The Gerecht Family Institute for Outreach now provides all rabbinical and cantorial students with a required three-day intensive training program on all aspects of conversion and outreach in congregational life. Working in a rich, long-term cooperative partnership with the URJ Department of Outreach and Membership, HUC-JIR has developed informal educational experiences that prepare students to face the ritual, educational, ideological, programmatic, and pragmatic questions that abound in congregational life in this important area. From the establishment of a welcoming atmosphere in congregations and the expansion of educational opportunities for those interested in exploring Jewish life, to questions of denominational acceptance of converts and the particular rituals that shape a person's entry into Judaism, students leave HUC-JIR with a far greater depth of vision and understanding of available resources in this critical area.

Our students now regularly participate in programs that help expand their view of the Jewish and religious worlds. Intra-faith activities sponsored by the Wexner Foundation and CLAL, plus a variety of interseminary discussion groups and other events, bring our students into closer contact with their Conservative, Orthodox, Reconstructionist, and otherwise affiliated or unaffiliated peers. Through coursework in comparative religion and during interfaith events jointly sponsored with Christian and Muslim organizations, our students are also exposed to diversity beyond the Jewish world, and have utilized this opportunity to befriend and learn from clergy and congregants of other faith groups—a key source of reflection and practical learning for their own professional lives.

A number of fellowships that are now available to students also highlight critical areas that require more attention within our educational universe. These fellowships represent investment by various foundations and the HUC-JIR in future leadership for the changed context. Our experience shows that enhanced educational experiences for selected students can positively influence the entire student body, helping important ideas permeate the whole community. The Mandel Fellowship supports students who choose to add a year of educational training to their rabbinical careers, incorporating study at the Mandel Centers at Brandeis and in Jerusalem in order to create rabbinical practitioners who are educationally savvy and ready to meet the needs of congregations hungry for learning at all levels. The Schusterman Rabbinical Fellowship pairs students from HUC-JIR with students from the Jewish Theological Seminary, and focuses directly upon questions of outreach and creating congregations that are welcoming and inclusive across denominational boundaries. The Tisch Fellowship prepares students who are interested in cutting-edge work in congregational settings, and benefits from much of the work in synagogue studies that our faculty has led over the past decade. Each of these fellowship programs highlights areas that are central to the creation of vibrant institutions of Jewish life. The combination of the three has led to far greater awareness of these issues across all our student bodies, both through the education of the fellows themselves and through their interaction with faculty and other students and programs sponsored for the community as well.

Pastoral Counseling and Healing

In the areas of health and pastoral counseling, tremendous advances have occurred in the recent past. On each of our American campuses, major centers have emerged that represent the very best of cutting-edge education and research in the field of pastoral work. Students at our Cincinnati campus benefit from the fact that HUC-JIR is the only Jewish seminary fully accredited for the rigorous and highly reflective Clinical Pastoral Education training program. In Los Angeles, the work of the Kalsman Institute on Judaism and Health creates awareness, resources, and training that help students learn about Jewish tradition's approach to health and healing, bioethics and pastoral care. In New York, the Blaustein Center for Pastoral Counseling offers faculty and students outstanding new approaches to learning and teaching about pastoral care, providing coursework, supervision and placements that broaden horizons and improve skills.

In Jerusalem, the Blaustein Center has also pioneered a number of programs that have introduced concepts of counseling to Israeli society in hospitals, the army, and other key venues that do not yet benefit from a full complement of counseling personnel or skills. This is a most promising development that has the potential to better integrate both counseling and Reform Judaism into the Israeli psyche in new and highly innovative ways. Whether here or in Israel, our students are completing their programs with greater counseling skills, deeper interest in counseling, and a far better understanding of supervision, referral, and counseling theory than ever before. These skills and enduring understandings will help students build communities more responsive to their congregants' emotional needs and enable them to craft better responses to the joyous and challenging moments clergy encounter with regularity—transforming functional responses to visionary opportunities.

The Future

While this is surely not an exhaustive account of the many, many innovations at work at the "new HUC-JIR," it does cover some of the major programs in progress. But what does the future hold? I will conclude with just the mention of a few areas of interest for the coming decade.

Technology

As more information moves online and online communities of meaning begin to be ubiquitous, what response will Judaism have to this new mode of relationships? HUC-JIR has already instituted a Jewish Studies Portal for its students and faculty that makes available thousands of primary and secondary textual resources for online study, preparation, and teaching. We are currently studying and experimenting with just how a seminary ought to build its online presence—and the implications for congregations and organizations—in this brave new world. The opportunities for teaching, learning, and research in this area are far beyond nascent now, and the potential is enormous to change the picture of how we function in the decade ahead.

Lifelong Learning

Programs run by our Distance Learning Department, the Experiment in Congregational Education, and the UJA-Federation of New York funded joint HUC-JIR/JTS Leadership Institute have long stressed building congregations and training professionals by encouraging learning at every point along the dual spectra of age and knowledge. HUC-JIR already encourages its students to consider themselves lifelong learners, and creates a trajectory of alumni study courses that can provide educational sustenance in their years as working professionals. In the years ahead, with the cooperation of the Union for Reform Judaism, I believe we need to consider the entire educational life cycle and develop enhanced opportunities and standards that enable our alumni to continue their study even as we enable congregants to become highly educated Reform Jews who are ready for leadership at all levels.

New Congregational Models

Many unaffiliated groups are experimenting with new sorts of congregational models. Local *minyanim, havurot,* and even Chabad represent alternative models of community that have all experienced some success. We need to understand better why these models sometimes thrive and what we can learn from them for our own future. In addition, we must reflect on the economic implications of synagogue membership and how that model must evolve to meet new American realities in the years ahead. What we learn must then be taught to our students and shared with the community to shape effective new models that enhance synagogue life.

Teambuilding

HUC-JIR is one of the few places in the world where students from the rabbinical, cantorial, education, and communal service programs study together. How can cooperative learning build teams of effective leaders who respect one another and lead, vision, manage, educate, and counsel in an integrated manner? What implications does this have for future clergy teams at work in synagogues and organizations? And what implications does it have for our modes of education?

Each of these areas (and many more beyond them) represents a unique and challenging question that HUC-JIR and our movement will engage in the years ahead.

Judaism has, after all, always believed in self-improvement: one need only look to the hopeful process of *heshbon hanefesh* and *teshu-vah* we each engage in annually to know that our tradition is predicated on the powerful idea that transformation is possible and challenging, but ultimately, valued and welcome. In engaging such questions, we will continue to transform ourselves and our community, reflect on what we do, and improve how we do it. It is such constant reflection and regular innovation that makes this moment at HUC-JIR so exciting and full of potential.

Agents of Change in an Emerging Field: A Conversation

Dru Greenwood

During the summer of 2008, five leaders of institutions that have either come into being or expanded in new ways since the mid-1990s in response to the drive for synagogue transformation "spoke" together via e-mail to reflect on their philosophy and practice. Rachel Cowan (NY89) is executive director of the Institute for Jewish Spirituality. Hayim Herring (JTS84) is executive director of STAR: Synagogue Transformation and Renewal. Robert Leventhal is senior consultant at The Alban Institute. Jonah Pesner (NY97) is founding director of Just Congregations at the Union for Reform Judaism. Rob Weinberg, Ph.D. is director of the Experiment in Congregational Education based at the Rhea Hirsch School of Education, HUC-JIR, Los Angeles. (More information about each program is available on their respective websites.[1])

Greenwood: This issue of the *CCAR Journal* focuses on synagogue transformation, terminology that took firm hold in the mid-1990s and that echoes today. Each of you is deeply involved in working with synagogues and synagogue leaders toward change. How would you define the kind of transformation you hope to see in the congregations with which you work? Is "transformation" the term you would use if you were starting your efforts today?

Weinberg: My work with the Experiment in Congregational Education is based on the premise that Jewish learning has the potential to transform the lives of Jews. The kind of transformation ECE seeks to support enables congregations to become communities of meaning

DRU GREENWOOD is director of SYNERGY: UJA-Federation of New York and Synagogues Together. In the interest of transparency it should be noted that UJA-Federation of New York is currently funding projects in New York headed by each of the participants in the conversation.

where what is learned is lived, where Jewish learning is not only about the head (knowing) but also about the hand (doing/living), the heart (believing/valuing), and the feet (belonging). To be that force for individual and communal transformation, congregations need continually to renew themselves, to innovate collaboratively and repeatedly in the direction of their own visions.

Pesner: Just Congregations' vision aims for transformation in a larger sense, starting from the individual, moving through the congregation, to the community and the larger world:

> Just Congregations engages Reform Jewish synagogues to act powerfully and successfully across lines of faith, class, and race to address the root causes of economic and social injustice. We nurture and train congregations to build deep relationships grounded in *Torah* and *avodah*/religious meaning within our member congregations, and foster authentic relationships with other communities who share a vision of a world redeemed. Our purpose is redemption: the sacred transformation of the world as it is—parched by oppression—into the world as we know it should be—overflowing with justice. (Vision statement: 2006)

As we think about transforming the world as it is into the world as it should be, we begin with the *synagogue* as it is, striving to be the *synagogue* as it should be. The assumption of congregation-based community organizing (the approach we teach) is that the power for change comes from organized people acting together. We teach synagogue leaders to build strong, deep networks of relationships inside their congregations and then across lines with members of other faith communities to act on their shared values and concerns. The primary tool of this work is the "relational meeting" in which folks tell their stories. Congregations conduct campaigns in which hundreds of relational meetings take place, framed with text study and rituals. In the process, synagogues move from being a series of programs to a community of relationships.

Cowan: At the Institute for Jewish Spirituality we start from a different place, playing a role in synagogue change through our work with rabbis, cantors, and lay leaders. Our belief is that significant change begins within the leaders—finding energy, hope, vision to see a bigger picture of what the congregation and its community could become, and then the courage to act. We believe that leaders cannot give to their people what they do not have themselves. Nor can they provide energy and vision when they are exhausted and burned out. So we begin by providing for them a safe contemplative environment where they have ample time to reflect, study, listen, pray, meditate, and work with their body in a sacred community. They emerge renewed, refreshed, re-inspired—with practices to help them continue to grow and to balance their lives. They also have a clearer vision of where they are going and what they are building.

We think this change is transformative when participants have not only learned skills and developed new program ideas, but have adopted new practices that enable them to continue to grow, to see their role differently, and to work in a deeper, more sustaining connection with God or a sense of *kedusha*. Leaders who are more deeply connected with their inner life can help make the communities' prayer more heartfelt and dynamic, can engage Jews with the questions of the meaning and purpose of their individual and collective lives, can model and inspire the communication between people so that staff and members listen, speak and act with respect, with *hesed* and *rahamim*, and can inspire the community to serve those who are in need of comfort, healing, food, and justice.

Leventhal: Transformation for me, reflected in my work with the Alban Institute, is also about leadership and the conversations and programs passionate leaders can engender. And, by the way, it's not dependent on whether a congregation is enjoying growth or shrinking in size. While my experience and Alban research argue that most boards and most clergy are managerial and functionary, we hope to provide skills and inspire leaders to connect their community, their traditions, and their context. Regardless of whether the community faces changes in demographics, life styles, affiliation, home practice, or competitors (shuls or soccer), transformational leaders re-envision their work in that place, reflect on their experience, and wrestle to make decisions and write the next leadership chapter. Leaders call others to this "writing project" with *hitlavut* (flame- fiery enthusiasm).This leadership passion is the opposite of the functionary and ordinary. These leaders ask what the meaning of their leadership is so that fellow members can go more deeply in their reflections about the meaning of their membership. Some congregations are blessed with an abundance of these passionate transformational lay and clergy leaders. Others are so broken, discouraged, and dysfunctional that they are not ready for consultation. I find that outside change consultants and facilitators can be particularly helpful with the majority that lies in the middle.

Herring: Leadership seems to be essential to all of us. I agree—transformation can't just be a "program." Rather, as I've seen through a number of STAR's initiatives, it's a mindset that must be shared by rabbis and volunteer leaders. A program or process can be the lever for the beginning of transformational change, but the greater challenge is to cultivate a way of permanent fresh thinking—something that does not always come naturally to synagogues, which are in the preservation, adaptation, and transmission business.

My vision of a synagogue that is transforming—and I prefer that construction—is one that grows with people as they evolve over time. Reveling in fresh perspectives, they create ongoing opportunities for involvement in which people of diverse backgrounds can participate. They understand that a Jewish community must also be part of the broader local community and the worldwide Jewish community. Respectful of the place of prayer, they also recognize that people have different ways to express and explore their Jewish selves and invite members and seekers to take advantage of multiple ways of doing so. While knowing what they stand for as a congregational community, they do not try to remake people in their image but invite them into the community and allow them to become who they are—transforming synagogues influence individuals and allow themselves to be influenced by others.

Greenwood: *How does the term "transformation" work for you? What other terms would you use to express your efforts?*

Herring: I'm not a fan of "transformation" for several reasons. As I mentioned before, it implies an endpoint instead of an ongoing process. It can also seem to imply that everything in the synagogue is broken and suggest a lack of respect in the relationship between the "transforming" agent and the synagogue—the object of the transformation. And finally, it promotes the idea that synagogues don't routinely change. While they often respond slowly to changes in the environment, some synagogues have been imaginatively adaptive on their own, without the help of external "transformation" efforts. On the other hand, there is an aspect of the term transformation that is worth remembering—it is lofty and idealistic. It implies a grand vision of the future, something often found lacking in synagogues, which by nature can run the risk of becoming parochial and focused on the routine.

Weinberg: To pick up on Hayim's point, I've noticed that "transformation" has garnered various reactions, including not a small amount of resentment, particularly from rabbis. It seems that some have heard the call for transformation as a criticism of their life's work as represented in their congregations as they are today. I don't believe it was ever intended that way. Nevertheless, when I have asked rabbis who were skeptical of the need for transformation whether they would, were they not its rabbi, choose to join their own congregation, tragically few have responded in the affirmative, suggesting a meaningful gap remains between the experience of congregational life in our best moments and our typical daily experience. Whether we like the word or not, transformational change—as distinguished from remedial, developmental, or transitional change—implies a journey of becoming, an ongoing change in identity and way of being—not just a change in the manner of doing. This is the kind of transformation the work of the Experiment in Congregational Education seeks to inspire and facilitate.

Cowan: The concept that more closely corresponds to our vision of synagogue change than "transformation" is "constant growth," not so much growth in numbers and budget—though they matter—but growth in consciousness toward ever closer alignment among purpose and vision and lived reality. By that I mean that a congregation continually works on itself, learning from experience, from teachers, from consultants, from other congregations, and from each other, what it means to become a place where people find connections to each other and to a sense of Jewish sacred purpose. Such change is not rapid, not sudden, but on-going—with ups and downs, meanderings, which are incremental and organic.

Greenwood: *What drew you to this work?*

Pesner: I grew up in a synagogue that taught me the meaning of community. When my father died young, my rabbi, youth advisers, and synagogue community surrounded me with love and mentoring. I became a rabbi because of that experience. Also, I grew up believing that synagogues should act on their values. I remember the night in the early 1980s during the beginning of the plague of homelessness, when the temple board voted to start a soup kitchen.

I was so proud that we were going to do something. Twenty-five years later, more people are poor, fewer have health care, schools are crumbling, and our synagogues are desperate to be effective in acting on our vision of a more just world. I developed the skills for congregation-based community organizing during my tenure at Temple Israel of Boston and feel compelled to bring both the vision and the skills to others to help make a difference.

Leventhal: We all bring our assumptions and life experiences to leading synagogue change. As a leader in my own community—I have been a federation campaign leader, a day school president, and a synagogue board member, I came with experience in manufacturing operations and entrepreneurial marketing. I'm goal oriented! I believed in the Jewish mission and I wondered how synagogues might improve. After reading Susan Shevitz's article "Organizational Theory"[2] on the characteristics of synagogues as organizations, I began to ask myself some tough questions. If congregations were so challenging to lead (pluralistic, loosely coupled, nonrational, etc.) and they did such a poor job of writing down their learning and institutionalizing their practices, how could they improve and step forward?

As I wrote in my book on synagogue visioning and planning,[3] we are all challenged to bring our special gifts to the building of the synagogue just as our ancestors brought their gifts *nedivut lev* (from the heart) to Bezalel for the desert *mishkan*. While not a scholar, I hoped I would be able to make a small (heartfelt) contribution to the field by developing a leadership story that could connect the ancient wisdom of our tradition, Alban research on healthy congregations, my management experience, and the practical realities of synagogue life to lead to some sustainable, helpful practices.

Weinberg: What drew me to this work was a combination of ideas, experiences, and relationships. Through a brief career in informal Jewish education in my college years, working at Olin-Sang-Ruby Union Institute, at Temple Beth El in Madison, Wisconsin and at Temple Israel of Minneapolis, I saw how powerful Jewish learning and living could be. I went on to build a career in organizational effectiveness and change consulting, which enabled me, in the early 1990s, to work with the faculty of the Rhea Hirsch School of Education on its long-range master plan, which led to the creation of ECE, and then later to consult to ECE on organizational change matters. By involving me in ECE and later recruiting me to lead it, Sara Lee and Isa Aron made it possible for me to integrate my values with my career skills. Their thoughtful approach, which looked beyond synagogue programs and individual leaders to systems and culture, was compelling. I saw that empowering everyday Jews to study text and to enter into visionary work had transformative power to engage individuals with Jewish living, to build a sense of community, and to establish collaborative, adaptive congregational cultures. At the time I became director, it had become clear that I could extend ECE's reach and expand its scope and impact.

Herring: It is difficult for me to separate my personal and professional feelings about synagogues. I was one of those shul kids who was fortunate to grow up in a congregation where a few elders and the cantor, *zichrono livracha* (who was also my uncle), knew how to make space for young people. By the time I was sixteen, I knew that the only way that I could possibly give back all the love and caring that I received from my synagogue was to become a congregational rabbi. I had the good fortune to serve a wonderful congregation for ten years and then to continue working with rabbis and synagogues, as well as with a broad array of federation partner organizations, before I came to STAR. So serving as STAR's first executive director was really an opportunity to spiral back to my essential interest in what I believe is still the primary identity-forming and mediating institution in the Jewish community today. When they work, synagogues have the potential to shape the lives of individuals and families spiritually, educationally, socially, and communally. A synagogue is one of the last remaining multi-generational places where young and old can meet and where, ideally, it doesn't matter who you are or what you do; you are accepted as an equal because each individual possesses the same divine spark. Synagogues can exemplify *ahavat yisrael*, a value that drew me to Jewish life as a teen and that animates the work that I do today.

Cowan: When I was growing up, my role model was Jane Addams. I wanted to build my own version of Hull House—space for people to learn and do so many vital things. When I first became involved in the revitalization of Ansche Chesed, a dying congregation on the Upper West Side of Manhattan, I saw that a synagogue was a Jewish version of a settlement house, only with religious aspirations as well. I loved the community, the conversations with elderly refugees and survivors, artists, young parents, some from traditional homes and some newly aroused seekers. People had such rich and varied stories. We could celebrate together, mourn together, comfort each other, share our children's growing up, take in the homeless. It showed me that a congregation can be an enormous source of meaning, healing, celebration, action in the world, strength, *hesed* and *ahavah*; that it can touch our lives in the dimension of head, heart, body, and soul. But such a congregation requires leadership that manifests those qualities and aspirations. That is why I chose to become a rabbi. Furthermore, now knowing many rabbis and cantors, I see how challenging their jobs are and how in need of renewal and care they are. They are forever nurturing others, so I want to create resources that sustain and inspire them.

Greenwood: *Is there an example of a congregation with which you've worked that stands out as emblematic of your vision of transformation?*

Leventhal: I recently worked with a congregation that had gone through several difficult rabbinic changes. At the same time, it had experienced an overall demographic downturn in its Jewish community, which was shrinking and aging. It began to tell what we call at Alban, the "problem saturated" story. Leaders lacked confidence since they had been blamed for problems with the staff and for the loss of membership. This reinforced a narrative of pessimism: "New ideas won't work here."

Offered the opportunity, the congregation engaged in a visioning and planning process, a new idea for it, through which it learned to celebrate its strengths and to become excited about its opportunities. This enthusiasm encouraged new people to join. They empowered their rabbi more. They began to think about the future. This led to a long overdue capital campaign. Even though the demographics of the community remain difficult, they began to tell a story of possibility. I find that some congregations are not ready to change, while others have extraordinary resources to engage in continuous improvement. Most, like this congregation, lie in the middle. New transformational leadership practices and programs can help them when they are ready.

Weinberg: To give a fair picture I must describe at least two congregations. One is a large and well-resourced congregation, the other one of modest size and means. The first has been actively experimenting, learning, innovating in pursuit of its vision for lifelong Jewish learning for well over a decade. It has innovated new models of learning for children and families, for adults, and for teens that touch lives in deep ways. It has redesigned its entire approach to Hebrew learning. Some new models have endured. Other experiments missed the mark and were brought to a close. When a regional economic downturn led the congregation to decide not to fill the position of a departing educator, two lay leaders stepped up to fill the role temporarily until the congregation could again afford professional leadership for that aspect of its educational program. Despite several change-overs in rabbinic, educational, and lay leadership over the years, the collaborative spirit of visionary innovation endures. Similar processes of visioning and experimentation have found their way into the worship and community aspects of congregational life.

The second congregation has been on this journey for about five years. Having tried new approaches on a small scale in early childhood, Shabbat family learning, and teen learning, the congregation passionately wanted to pursue its vision of Jewish learning as a "partnership among the generations and between the synagogue community and its members." The leadership of this congregation is committed to fostering positive experiences for children with adults in the community. It wants children to have the kind of Jewish "neighborhood" experience that no longer exists along the lanes and avenues where children actually live. It chose to embark on a bold experiment it calls the Kehillah model, which divides the entire congregation into smaller groups of mixed ages that live in diverse areas and that meet at least six times during the year for a Shabbat celebration, a *tikkun olam* activity, or a holiday celebration. Through these *kehillot*, says the senior rabbi, "We're trying to replicate the serendipity of relationships that happened when we were a congregation of a hundred families." Having applied unsuccessfully for grants to fund the Kehillah model, the congregation made a difficult, vision-driven decision to discontinue isolated "one-shot" family education and other programs, and instead to re-align its modest resources and commit clergy and staff time to realizing the model that best aligned with its vision.

Both congregations articulated a compelling vision for Jewish learning and community that would touch the Jewish lives of congregants in serious and positive ways. Each congregation's leaders work together—experimenting, learning, refining, and making choices (sometimes difficult ones)—to bring its vision closer to reality.

Herring: I have also watched many synagogues begin the road to transformation, but there is one that I'll comment on because, of the almost 200 Synaplex synagogues, I'm very familiar with it. Synaplex came at the perfect time for this congregation. It was a smaller congregation that wanted and needed to grow its membership and deepen the sense of congregational community. Now, about five years later, this congregation has developed a guiding vision that is like the soul of the congregation; it permeates the community. It has put energy and thought into *tefillah*, making it inspirational and multi-generational. The number of individuals and families who participate both on Shabbat and at other times during the week has increased dramatically. Welcoming is embedded into its services and activities. A substantial number of new volunteers are involved in planning, and veteran volunteers serve as mentors to acculturate them, while still respecting their new ideas. A culture of assessment and reflection on key programs and activities has been established, ensuring alignment with the mission of the congregation. The congregation has increased its capacity to fund its dreams and improved its ability to plan long term. Its membership has grown and it has already begun to think about the next steps on the path of growing as a vibrant congregation, exploring taking part in congregation-based community organizing.

The role the rabbi chose to play was critical throughout this process of change. Using the Synaplex supports to open the synagogue system to experimentation, this rabbi also found the right balance between leading and creating space for others to be involved in re-envisioning what this congregation could become. Throughout the journey, this rabbi inspired confidence in the volunteer leadership, celebrated achievements, and was personally secure in understanding that it was more important to aspire to become the community that it could be than to attempt to imitate others' ideas of what "success" was.

On a personal note, I intentionally visited the congregation on a Synaplex Shabbat with my daughter, who was a high school junior at the time. *Tefillot* as she had experienced them in several settings had the unfortunate effect of really turning her off. I knew that if she accompanied me to this congregation, which had great, soulful music and an atmosphere of joy and meaning, I had a chance to expose her to a totally different kind of worship experience. Although she was familiar with the liturgy, I noticed that she was not participating. When I asked her why, she responded, "Abba, they have smiles on their faces. This service is awesome." My daughter is now a sophomore in college (teaching at a Reform religious school in Boulder) and a few weeks ago once again referred to how this experience was pivotal in helping her understand that there are congregations that can make her feel at home. I am indebted to the congregation for helping a searching teenager find an oasis of Jewish meaning and I'm sure that many people who have walked through those synagogue doors can tell similar stories.

Pesner: Although congregation-based community organizing has a long track record particularly in the church world, Just Congregations is only a few years old. The first "Just Congregation" that we worked with is Congregation B'nai Jehoshua Beth Elohim (BJBE) in Glenview, Illinois. Under the leadership of then Associate Rabbi John Linder and a team of lay leaders, the congregation launched *Panim El Panim*, a campaign in which hundreds of members participated in one-on-one relational meetings. They studied text, shared their stories, and celebrated their commitment to strengthening the ties of their community. During the process at BJBE, one member shocked the community when she shared for the first time in public that she and her family lost their business because of competition from a new "big-box" store, and were living with no health insurance. BJBE leaders have been able to fill buses on a regular basis to head to the statehouse and join members of churches, mosques, and other communities through United Power for Action and Justice in a successful fight to increase health care access in Illinois. The political victory has meant that BJBE is a congregation that effectively acts on its values. But it is also a place that strives to value relationships more than programs.

Cowan: In keeping with the mission of the Institute for Jewish Spirituality, I share a different kind of example. What follows is the reflection of a rabbi who was transformed by his experience with the Institute for Jewish Spirituality. From this place he will not only develop new programs, but will give more relevant sermons, intensify the davening, and inspire his congregants to think bigger, to imagine more creatively, and build a stronger, richer congregation.

> My understanding of my role in the world as a rabbi has been completely transformed as a result of my practice. Once upon a time, the rabbinate held promise for me as a "title," a source of authority and influence, and a deepening of egoic self-identi-

fication. Now, that "title" has turned itself upside down in my experience. If I have any purpose, it's "to be the Torah of Transforming the World through Opening the Heart." Again, this is meant as the opposite of narcissism. It means that in moments when I have the strength and courage to open my heart to the Truth, however frightening that Truth may seem, that Truth then reveals itself to be Torah. And in that open-hearted Awareness, the whole world is transformed. Suddenly it's not that I'm the rabbi and "they" are the congregants. . . . When they put me on a bimah in front of them and ask me to "teach them" Torah, I discover that I am only a mirror, reflecting the radiance of Torah I discover in the texts, in their hearts, in the moment.

Greenwood: *What is the greatest barrier you see to synagogue change? How has a congregation or congregational leader you've worked with overcome it?*

Pesner: The gravitational pull of the "synagogue as it is" away from our dream of the "synagogue as it should be" at times feels immense. Very often, rabbis, staff, and lay leaders fall back on programs, projects, and activities. I don't remember my childhood temple's programs; I remember the network of people who cared for me when my father died. I remember the kids I sat with on the bus to Washington. I remember the song leader who turned me on to being Jewish.

Spending the time to truly invest in training leaders; slowly building relationships; being patient with a deep process that engages a broad-base of members; conducting regular reflection and evaluation—this is all much harder than running a slick program. But at the end of the day, as we are taught in *Pirke Avot*, "according to the labor is the reward."

Cowan: The greatest barrier to overcoming the inertia and resistance to change is lack of organization, backup, and strategy. It leads to demoralization, when people try something for which they are not prepared and too readily conclude they have failed. Having experienced such failure, I learned an extremely effective approach to success. As co-chair of the Social Action committee at Congregation B'nai Jeshurun in Manhattan, I learned the methodology that Jonah Pesner describes above.

As we worked to overcome the resistance to changing the ineffective ways the social action committee had tried to involve the wider community in social action, we adopted the congregation-based community-organizing approach modeled by Temple Israel in Boston. We deliberately brought it slowly and gently into the life of the congregation, building support first with the rabbis, then the Board, and then with the wider community through a series of 613 one-on-one conversations and house meetings. Toward the beginning of the process a new staff member was hired to coordinate the organizing, and to integrate it into the work of the Board. The result is the integration of the CBCO model into the life of the congregation, leading to three *hevras* that are each responsible for a different advocacy campaign—relating to the environment, marriage equality, and participation in a city-wide interfaith coalition; three members of the organizing task force who now sit on the Board; and the pattern of community organizing, relationship building, and outreach being adopted by other committees of the synagogue.

Weinberg: One of the greatest barriers is timidity of leadership, the tendency to succumb to inertia rather than courageously imagining a different future and taking chances large and small to bring it into being. This barrier results in small changes with vanishing effects.

I have seen congregations overcome it by daring to dream, by using the tools the process has given them (e.g., a vision) to guide a journey and to motivate people to join in personally and financially. I've seen other congregations overcome it by remaking the systems that made it hard to change in the first place (such as the economic model of synagogues and congregational education) and by making tough choices in line with vision, e.g., to stop doing certain things or to expect more of congregants (even at risk of disappointing someone) in order to devote resources to bringing their vision to life.

Herring: I hate to reference an anti-Semite, but Henry Ford is alleged to have said: "if you think you can do a thing or you think you can't do a thing, you're right." A true belief in the possibility of change, that things can be fundamentally different from what they are at present, is one of the keys to making change happen. I don't want to simplify the answer to this question and suggest that everything comes down to attitude, but many people unconsciously hold themselves prisoners to their own aspirations and that's true of institutions as well. Maintaining belief in a fundamentally different outcome, in the face of people who will explain why things really can't change, provides that necessary boost over the barriers to change that others intentionally or unintentionally create. Like my colleagues, I worry about the gravitational pull that seems to take bold ideas and bring them down to a more mundane level in the name of consensus.

There is a famous talmudic story in which a group of sages forget an obscure Jewish law or *halakha* because of the infrequency in which it is applicable. While discussing what the law should be, one of them recommends, "go out to the market place and see how the people are behaving." I value this story because it reminds me that in addition to the wisdom that Jewish professionals possess, there is a lot of wisdom in the Jewish street as well. Paying attention to the marketplace was good advice then. It is equally valuable today.

Leventhal: To me, the biggest barrier also has to do with leadership: the lack of a large guiding coalition for change. If I can help this coalition form, I have partners for the change process. When they become a team, change has begun. While your situation may seem unique and your challenges complex, you have control over one thing: your leadership response to the opportunities of your mission and your moment. Commit to create a guiding coalition and a leadership conversation. Something will stir and God will help provide the courage and wisdom you need to write a hopeful story about the congregational community of your dreams.

Greenwood: *What advice do you have for synagogue leaders considering embarking on a significant congregational change initiative? And what do you hope leaders will look for in extra-congregational support?*

Cowan: My advice for synagogue leaders would be to be sure, first, that the process they begin includes time for community-building and self-renewal within the leadership group—sharing of passions, interests, stories, texts, and prayer—and a plan to widen the circle of change agents in a continuous way through campaigns of one-on-one conversations that increase the number of relationships within the congregation. Another key: assure that their rabbi and cantor are closely involved and mutually supportive. Patience and mutual support will be vital, as the process will take a long time, and have many ups and downs. Assign a staff member to work with them to hold/organize the process.

I hope that synagogues will look for extra-congregational support in several places: a consultant trained in congregational change; a network of congregations engaged in change processes from whom they can learn and with whom they can exchange experiences; and start-up funding so they can staff the process. And finally, that the leaders, both professional and lay, will set aside time to cultivate their inner lives so that they bring spiritual qualities of patience, compassion, clear-sightedness, and optimism to their work, building sacred community as they go.

Weinberg: I would expand on that a bit. In working with an outside consultant, congregations should look for a process that helps define, clarify, and articulate its own vision and goals and to bring those together with lay and professional partners to emerge with a shared vision. Further, the approach should view the congregation in a holistic, systemic way and seek to appreciate, affirm, and strengthen the best of what the congregation is, does, and values, rather than only finding or seeking problems to solve. (An analogy to working toward wellness vs. finding and curing sickness is illustrative.)

My advice in considering whether or not to begin? For rabbis particularly, make sure you are ready; all transformation is first personal. If you are not ready to reflect and entertain deep change yourself in how you do things, how you think about your rabbinate and your relationships with your staff and lay partners, don't start. Yes, have patience; long-lasting, far-reaching, significant and deep change that touches lives and alters institutional culture doesn't happen from one Shabbat to the next. Be prepared to stick with it, devoting your passion, time, attention, and personal "capital" for a minimum of five years and probably longer to see the results you seek. Be prepared to both lead and listen. When you are committed and prepared, and you have successfully engaged the imaginations of the members of your congregational community, do not hesitate to think big and act boldly.

Herring: When you've chosen to begin, remember that perfection belongs to God, so don't worry if all of the details of whatever change you plan to make are not precisely developed. While not serving as an excuse for lack of planning, it's preferable to launch a change initiative with 80% of the plan ready and allow the remaining details to emerge, gaining clarity through the work of implementation. Question the wisdom of reaching for the "low hanging fruit." You can spend months or even years reaching for incremental change, which frustrates those with greater expectations as well as those who really like things the way they are. So while it's helpful to have a few "quick wins," aim higher, dream more and start to give life more immediately to some of those larger dreams. During your initial dreaming, suspend your disbelief in what you think is impossible and surround yourself with enough people who sincerely believe that your congregation is capable of creating what it can dream. Don't worry—later on, enough people will be available to critique your dream and shape it into the realities of your context. Build on your strengths, invite new people into the process, celebrate your successes, be optimistic when temporary setbacks occur and allow enough time for the change to take root in your congregation. In other words, do not fall into the trap of having congregational Attention Deficit Disorder (A.D.D.), but stick with your plans until you see them bear fruit. Assess, reflect, and communicate throughout the process and remember to celebrate along the way!

Leventhal: I agree! I would rather have a goal that is only 80% right than no goal. The goal that is only 80% on target will stimulate debate, it will get worked, it will evolve, and if leaders are wrong they can change course. At least they have done something to close the gap between their aspirations and their current practice.

Starting a significant synagogue change initiative calls for a number of strategies from the outset:

1. Create a sense of urgency for change. This means heightening awareness of the gap between your vision and your practice.
2. Provide a hopeful vision—to replace "the problem saturated story"—of how change can make a difference, and a practical road map people can believe in.
3. Help make the board more strategic and visionary so it can manage change. Help the board learn to empower strategic task forces to address transformational opportunities (social justice, advanced adult education, innovative worship, community building, Synaplex, etc.) and support their experiments. It is hard for a non-strategic board to welcome strategic work.
4. As my colleagues have suggested, build a large guiding coalition of task force members and board leaders to champion the change process. There will be resistance to pointing out weaknesses or investing in new approaches. The support of the board and the planning committee prevents the plan from being identified with one person.

5. Start with guiding principles. Don't rush to problem solving because that is where conflict emerges.

6. Ensure that there are new people in the process.[4] It is hard for the same people who have been part of the "problem satu-rated story" to write a new one. Some new writers are needed.

7. Prepare leaders to make the investment of time and money for the 12 to 24-month journey. They need to role model stam-ina and commitment in order to finish the script.

Pesner: In advising a synagogue considering change, I assume that a congregation is ultimately a group of people, collective stakehold-ers in a community, as opposed to an institution. Therefore, I too think that the critical first step is to assemble the right leadership team. I see several essential questions to consider: Who are the appropriate leaders in the congregation who have a strong network of relationships that reach deeply into the congregation, who will be able to listen well and then engage a broad-base of members in the change process? Then, what is the training those leaders need to be effective? Next, the leadership team needs to ask, what is the collec-tive strategy to engage the community broadly? Finally, the team needs to establish a clear mechanism for accountability, asking: Is the process time-bound, with clear goals, and regular periods of reflection and evaluation?

Greenwood: It is perhaps appropriate to end, as we started, with questions. Thank you all very much.

Notes

1. The Institute of Jewish Spirituality: www.ijs-online.org/; STAR: Synagogues: Transformation and Renewal: www.starsynagogue. org; The Alban Institute: www.alban.org; Just Congregations: www. urj.org/justcongregations/; The Experiment in Congregational Education: www.ECEonline.org.

2. Isa Aron, Sara Lee, and Seymour Rossel, editors, *A Congregation of Learners* (Union for Reform Judaism Press, 1995).

3. Robert Leventhal, *Stepping Forward: Synagogue Visioning and Planning* (Alban Institute, 2008).

4. Jim Collins, *Good to Great* (New York, Harper Collins Publishers, 2001).

Making Change in the *Kehillah*

Deborah Joselow

Some form of the Hebrew word *"kehillah"* appears in the Bible close to one hundred different times. With this as an inspiration, I arrived to serve my first congregation. I anticipated many things from my study of the Jewish concept of community. My practical experiences prior to ordination only added to my expectations. I understood the synagogue as a basic building block of American Jewish life and the chance to live in and work with a fundamental piece of the equation seemed as much as any rabbi could want.

My definition of community was anchored in three overlapping principles: (1) the world could be changed; (2) human beings (every single one of us) were the agents of progress; and (3) working in tandem with one another and with God, we could make repairs. During my years at Temple Emanuel in Westfield, New Jersey, in all that I did I tried to find a way to empower all voices, whether they lived at the center or at the margins. I also came to understand that my own role as a pulpit rabbi gave me a unique voice, one that I had to learn to use with equal amounts of care and confidence. My own dream was to enhance the rich fabric of the place that had asked me to serve and to leave them—and myself—stronger and more vital by virtue of having nurtured new conversations.

When I came to work at UJA-Federation of New York, I expected to have my understanding of *kehillah* enhanced by the change in altitude. I recalibrated my lens and prepared for what this new perch could teach me. I had spent the first years of my rabbinate living with a local focus. Now I was prepared to see the world through a global kaleidoscope. I traded taglines, moving from underneath Micah's banner of "to do justly, to love mercy and walk humbly with God"

DEBORAH JOSELOW (NY91) is managing director of the Commission on Jewish Identity and Renewal at UJA-Federation of New York.

into a place that proclaimed its intent to "care for those in need, rescue those in harm's way and renew Jewish life," but frankly the vision seemed the same. In some ways the world did get bigger and more complex. But the belief in the power of the collective, whether in a community of one million or a community of a few hundred, is very much the same endeavor. I have different resources, but the values being applied at 59th Street and in Westfield are identical.

People sometimes ask me why I left the congregational rabbinate to work at UJA-Federation. The question has never made any sense to me. To put it plainly, I have and do see synagogues and federations as two sides of the same coin. Although each organization may have a distinct language and culture, we share a mission, vision, and purpose. This makes us, in my mind, colleagues. I was, and remain, one of only three rabbis at UJA-Federation of New York. However I did not check my *smicha* at the door when I came here. Rather, I accepted the premise that in hiring a rabbi, UJA-Federation blessed my skill sets and desired me to apply my rabbinic sensibilities in everything that I did.

A central part of the mandate of UJA-Federation is that doing our work means empowering other agencies that share our vision and have the potential to deliver on critical communal strategies. As I explain my job to my children, obviously in jest, I tell them that I don't actually work in an organization that does anything. In large part UJA-Federation of New York marks success by the strength and vitality of the Jewish community outside our building. Our *kehillah* is represented by organizations and institutions that all of us call home, places such as day schools, synagogues, and camps, family service, hospitals, and nursing homes that embrace the full spectrum of our needs and aspirations. This is the world that UJA seeks to nurture and sustain.

The official catchment of UJA-Federation of New York is the five boroughs of New York City, the counties of Long Island and Westchester, Israel, the former Soviet Union, and the rest of the world. This is a dynamic and varied terrain. Even for an organization as large as UJA-Federation, the size and scope of our mandate make it difficult to fully embrace all the people and places offering an opportunity to participate in Jewish life. Although my rabbinic colleagues in the field may have a more regular opportunity to interface with individual members of the Jewish community, my UJA colleagues and I seek to serve these same individuals even from afar. Within the walls of our building we may not offer housing, meals, or daycare, but the face of each need fuels our pursuit. Caring, peoplehood, and Jewish education are simultaneous endeavors for us. And while this tri-partite agenda may complicate things, we, like Kohelet, believe that the three-fold cord not quickly broken is both the Jewish past and future.

Much of the time we choose to invest in strengthening the infra-structure of Jewish life. This is a slow and sometimes overwhelming task. With so many pressing and acute needs, it can be hard to convince people (even me) to be patient while the wisdom and capacity are evolving. Although this is not the easiest short-term route, this strategy of community building is critical to a viable and vibrant long-term future. It is also a piece of the landscape that we inhabit alone. Except in very small ways, no other major Jewish organization makes a regular or significant commitment to the physical and intellectual capital of Jewish community. Even with a campaign of nearly $200 million annually, resources must be applied with discretion.

But we also have the ability to be enormously creative and it is this opportunity for artistry that drew me to my work. Challenges that are so large and complex demand new ways of thinking and acting. The benefit of maintaining an ideology that transcends any single denomination is that UJA-Federation can cast a wide net in seeking solutions to joint problems. In my seven years of work, I have been blessed to witness the most unlikely of partnerships. There is nothing quite as gratifying as the transformation of strang-ers and even adversaries into neighbors. When UJA-Federation of New York succeeds, that is exactly what we are all able to witness. I have many examples of this movement but the one that I have watched for the longest time is our work in supplementary educa-tion.

In my corner of UJA-Federation of New York when I began in my position, several issues had been simmering for too long. In partic-ular there were deep concerns about supplementary religious education (often called "afternoon Hebrew school"), the setting in which most children in the United States receive their primary and only Jewish education. Change certainly required us to reach out to partners in the synagogue world. As we (professionals and volun-teer leaders) traveled around New York with our aspirations, we were met with a certain amount of incredulity. No one doubted our intentions; they all just seemed dubious of our outreach to them. I was well prepared for the content conversations, but the skepticism was a bit of a personal and professional shock. My very wise family doctor taught me that most human beings can grow in only one direction at a time. I certainly appreciate that the trajectory of UJA-Federation may not always be in sync with those whom we need to help us reach our goals, but I did not anticipate that I would need to convince the synagogue world of our credentials.

Today as we seek to move the needle of congregational education, we enjoy positive and productive relationships with Hebrew Union College, the Jewish Theological Seminary, our central agencies for Jewish education, and dozens of congregations and congregational professionals. It was not a simple or straight road from there to here and plenty of strands remain to be woven. In truth, our agenda in supplemental Jewish education is still evolving. While the pace and level of funding may frustrate all of us who now occupy the same table, the fact that we can openly share our disappointments and successes is a tribute to the strength of what has been built. The issue of quality part-time Jewish education did not belong to UJA-Federation, but representatives of this organization can claim to have elevated the conversation so it is now accepted as a communal aspiration. We are in the early stages, but there is no doubt that by virtue of pursuing this together, by jointly sharing assets, we have changed things far beyond the classroom. I use this progress in one sliver of Jewish life as a mantra on days when the complexities of my work resemble a Gordian knot.

This issue of the *CCAR Journal* is devoted to synagogue transformation. I accept the criticism that comes from using this headline. While it may read as a critique of life in a congregation, in fact it is meant as an expression of an ideal. For Abraham and Sarah, *kehillah* was expressed as hospitality. In my view in today's world, we need this big tent now more than ever. If synagogue and federation professionals could together hold those flaps open to the heavens, imagine what kinds of miracles would come flooding in.

A Philadelphia Story: Partnership for Change

Philip Warmflash

"Sure we always find someone to help for the food pantry or the Purim carnival, but they won't even consider taking a position on the board."

"We just can't find anyone who wants to be the president; now we're trying to find two or three people to share the job before we ask a past president to step in."

"How do I get the board to understand that it's not just about numbers—it's relationships?"

When I first came to Philadelphia fifteen years ago to direct the Jewish Outreach Partnership, then called Community Hebrew Schools, I would never have expected to hear, let alone address, these kinds of concerns. At that time the agency was a Federation-supported supplementary school for the unaffiliated, an educational institution that also created special outreach programs targeting those (including "under-affiliated") who could not find their place in a synagogue. The story of JOP's evolution from those early days, when synagogue leaders looked on JOP's role with distrust, to today, when our work focuses mostly on assisting local Philadelphia-area congregations on synagogue strengthening, is its own saga of transformation, which I leave for another day.

JOP's longevity in the community, however, and our transformation to the central address for synagogue leaders in the Philadelphia area to look for education and consultation came from synagogue leaders feeling empowered when they participated in JOP programs. Gradually, through the auspices and support of our local Jewish Federation, JOP has become the 4-1-1 and the 9-1-1 for more than 60 synagogues in three states.

PHILIP WARMFLASH (JTS'81) is executive director of Jewish Outreach Partnership in Philadelphia.

Now these questions from synagogue leaders—the deep questions about membership engagement, volunteer commitment, and the future of our synagogue communities—are the questions that JOP addresses regularly. And, in keeping with our name and mission, understood in a new way, partnership and education remain the keystones to our approach.

The Tuttleman Leadership Institute

In the spring of 2007, JOP was given a challenge that was, in fact, a gift for our own learning and development. The request came from Steven Wernick, rabbi of a Conservative synagogue in suburban Philadelphia. Could JOP create a high-quality leadership development program that would attract and inspire Gen-Xers in his synagogue to become more engaged and to consider taking leadership roles in the coming years? Rabbi Wernick was interested in an initiative that could serve as a foundation for creating a new model of synagogue leadership and a new level of partnership with the rabbi. He was certain that he could secure funds for this project from one of the families in the congregation. And with that my staff and I got to work to identify the key components for what would become the Tuttleman Leadership Institute (TLI).

The vision of TLI training is that effective synagogue leadership will be a personally transforming, meaningful Jewish experience in which individuals view their volunteer work as *avodat ha-kodesh*, a sacred task, through which a *kehillah kedosha*, a holy community, can be built. Further, synagogue leaders will feel that their volunteer work is linked to Jewish learning, Jewish values, and Jewish life, balancing personal reflection about one's own Jewish journey with learning about contemporary organizational-development theory and making decisions that reflect both.

From this vision we identified the key elements of TLI. The TLI Fellows would be a small group of no more than a dozen, and participants would be required to complete an application that included a reflective essay about their Jewish life. To deepen the sense of the serious commitment to the group, TLI would encompass eight three-hours sessions over the year. Each would begin with dinner and a check in, followed by intensive text study and case studies. Finally, in addition to the eight sessions of the program each TLI fellow would be asked to incorporate a new Jewish practice of their choosing into their lives while in the program; this new practice would be identified through personal meetings of the Fellow with Rabbi Wernick twice during the year.

The most difficult and critical component of TLI was creating a curriculum and planning the flow of each session to move the multi-layered process forward. To effectively reach our target population, we had to balance personal meaning and growth with a sense of *brit* and communal obligation. Further, while we knew this would be a highly educated group generally, the level of Jewish learning would be uneven. Most had little or no experience studying Jewish texts as adults. To make the Jewish learning explicit, we decided that each of the eight three-hour sessions would be based on a *midah*, a value concept. That *midah* would be amplified through the study of a traditional text and would serve as a lens for the discussion of that evening's leadership concept.

The opening sessions focused squarely on individual needs and not on the needs of the synagogue, highlighting the concepts of *tzelem elohim* (the image of God) and *anavah* (humility) and exploring leadership in the lives of each Fellow. From the personal, individual, we were able to move fairly easily into leadership challenges, including team-building, conflict resolution, communications, and developing systems through the lenses of *gevurah* (strength), *ka'as* (anger), *savlanut* (patience), *kavod* (honor), *zerizut* (readiness), and ending, as we had started, with *tzelem elohim*.

Perhaps the most innovative aspect of TLI is the rabbi's central role in its implementation. Although Rabbi Wernick knew that he did not have the time in his schedule to fully develop and implement this project, he realized that JOP could serve as the vehicle through which he could shape and actualize his vision of synagogue leadership. While JOP is responsible for the curriculum and much of the teaching, the rabbi is a full partner. Through his constant presence at each session and individual consultation with each participant, he modeled the ideal role of spiritual leader of a congregation. He was the person in the room who brought this group of Tuttleman Fellows together, and who valued each of the participants. He was not afraid to share actual synagogue issues with them or to respond to challenging questions with honesty and humanity. For most, if not all the fellows, this made TLI unlike any experience they had ever had in a synagogue and with a rabbi.

In the fall of 2007, when the ten participants in the first Tuttleman Leadership Institute entered the room, it was clear that they were not sure what they had gotten themselves into. Within the first hour of being together, as they began to explore *tzelem elohim* and linking that concept to their lives, the change in the room was palpable. Without exaggeration, all these people, most of whom had limited exposure to Jewish texts, found that they had a deep hunger for study and an accessible teacher and guide in their rabbi.

Over the year the TLI Fellows became a cohesive group that felt a new connection to each other and to their synagogue community. They had a high-level, personally engaging, challenging experience that enabled them to cultivate their Jewish knowledge and their sense of themselves as leaders. At the closing gathering of this first cohort, participants spoke of being transformed, about wanting to be life-long Jewish learners, and about seeing their role in guiding their synagogue into the future. They were also unanimous in their commitment to continue meeting as a group during the year. We, who directed the program, felt as if we had planted the seeds that, with nurturing, could grow a new model of synagogue leader.

It is now fall, 2008. JOP is beginning year two of the Tuttleman Leadership Institute with a new group of participants and a second level that will bring experienced synagogue leaders in as "Partners" for last year's group. We have also begun year one of the Presidents' Leadership Institute at another synagogue where the past presidents have provided major support for training their leaders of the future.

JOP continues to offer support and consultation to the synagogues across this region. So what have we at JOP learned from our years of doing this work? Institutionally we have learned that there is great power and potential in being and agency with an ongoing mission and a local presence. We have learned that it takes time to build and nurture relationships of trust and support with rabbis and synagogues and that only in that way are we able to jointly build institutional strength and to create opportunities for transformation. We feel like we have discovered and continue to refine an integrated way of working in the community and with its congregations in authentic Jewish ways, in ways that increase a sense of *kehillah kedoshah*, of holy, inspired, community, and in ways that will continue to build visionary congregations.

Future of the Synagogue

Amy L. Sales

The 1939 World's Fair offered to the public the World of Tomorrow. Ironically, the exhibit did not accurately predict the future but it did say much about the present at that time, and correctly suggested that "familiarity with today is the best preparation for the future." In similar fashion, we cannot know the synagogue of the future, but we can imagine the possibilities by understanding the present trends that are pushing on the institution.

The one certitude is that the future will be different from the present. The history of the American synagogue—the immigrant *shtiebel* giving way to the urban synagogue and then the suburban "shul with a pool"—illustrates the constancy of change.[1] The story of the *havurah* movement or Moshe House demonstrates that new organizational forms can be created for worship, study, and action.

The question about the future of the synagogue is not just about its form but its vitality. From a sociological perspective, vitality rests on the capacity of the institution to engage "twenty- and thirty-somethings."[2] They are the next generation and *ipso facto* it is they who will comprise the future that we are trying to predict today.

Form is a characteristic of the *synagogue*, a term that refers to the organization's structure—its physical plant, professional staff, programs, governance, and all the concerns that come under the rubric of the business of the synagogue. Vitality is a characteristic of the *congregation*, a term that refers to the human system—the people who inhabit this place and their connections to one another.[3] Along with the rabbinate, these components comprise the institution we commonly refer to as "the synagogue." The premise here is that the future will be determined by the environmental factors affecting the

AMY L. SALES, Ph.D. is Associate Director of the Cohen Center for Modern Jewish Studies at Brandeis University, Waltham, Massachusetts.

synagogue, the socio-demographic factors affecting the congregation, and the rabbinic responses to these. Although every synagogue is subject in one way or another to these same forces, we focus here primarily on American Reform congregations.

The Changing Synagogue

Although they have been slow to recognize themselves as such, synagogues are part of the nonprofit sector. In recent years, this sector has been marked by an increasing emphasis on professionalism, efficiency, fund-raising, and competition, and these trends are unlikely to diminish in the coming years.

Faced with growing technical, legal, and operational complexity, nonprofit agencies have embraced business methods and professional management. Increasingly, they are turning from lay volunteers to professionals to direct core functions. Key among these functions is fund-raising. Pressured by organizational growth, rising costs, and cuts in public funding, nonprofits have come to appreciate the need for greater effectiveness in fund-raising and financial resource development. Their attention is turning, as well, to increased efficiency, for example, by greening the organization (both as a cost savings and as an appeal to public sentiments), establishing collaborations among smaller nonprofits, and outsourcing functions handled more efficiently elsewhere.

Within this climate, the role of lay leadership is necessarily changing. More attention is being paid to good governance, fiscal stewardship, and strategy. Importantly, board members are being asked to shift their focus from day-to-day operations to the future of the agency and its strategic direction. This shift has not come easily to synagogue boards where the organization is often seen more as "extended family" and less as not-for-profit agency. Nonetheless, the conversations suggested by this journal are exactly the kinds of conversations that smart boards are having.

Not including congregations, there are over 3.5 million charitable nonprofits in the United States and this number is growing annually. The result is increased competition in the search for professional talent, top lay leadership, and donors—all of whom have ample opportunity to give their gifts elsewhere. Difficulties in finding a qualified development director or administrator are not reflective of an inept or unlucky synagogue but of the reality affecting the entire not-for-profit sector.

Within the synagogue world we can therefore expect to see shifting lay and professional roles and expectations, increasing fundraising needs, and growing competition for talent and dollars. The successful synagogue will need to respond to these trends with good organizational and business sense.

The Changing Congregation

The synagogue is not just an operational system. It is also a deeply human system whose primary concern is its members; their Jewish lives, learning, and aspirations; and their connections to one another. Over the course of the past two generations, liberal American Jewry has become more secular and individualist in its orientation. This trend, often accompanied by low levels of Jewish education, has left young American Jews with a poor understanding of religious beliefs and ideology. Weak Judaic knowledge, values, and beliefs challenge the future vitality of the synagogue and raise the question of whether or not the rising generation will join synagogues and, if so, what kind of institution they will require.

The Knowledge Challenge

Demographic shifts over the past generation have resulted in large numbers of children being raised in intermarried families. This experience does not determine adult choices but the consequent Jewish social networks and education do. The Jewish density of an individual's high school social network and the level of Jewish education received growing up are both strong predictors of the importance that an individual will place on being Jewish as an adult. Jewish education growing up also predicts adult Jewish behaviors, including ritual practice and synagogue affiliation.[4]

The greater the education through the teenage years, the greater the likelihood of joining a congregation in adulthood. The level of Jewish education among Reform-raised young adults, however, is low, both absolutely and relative to other groups. They tend to end their formal education at a young age and do not necessarily recommence Judaic learning in college. Indeed, our study of American college students found that those who consider themselves Reform Jews were the least Jewishly engaged of any group, including those with no denominational identity.[5]

The link between education and affiliation suggests that, unchecked, the rising generation is likely to eschew synagogue membership and those who do join may be less ready to contribute to the Judaic richness of the congregation. This prediction is heightened by expected changes in denomination switching. Over the past generation, many raised in the Conservative movement switched into Reform congregations, adding to the membership a cadre with more intensive Jewish educational backgrounds.[6] Given the shrinkage in the Conservative movement, this inflow is likely to slow in the future. The Reform movement will therefore need to rely even more heavily on its "homegrown" population to build its congregations.

The Values and Belief Challenge

Although much has been written about the rising generation, there is little systematic data about Jewish 20- and 30-somethings. The general rule is that Jews are just like other Americans only more secular. Whatever our analysis, we must take a strong dose of secularity as a given.

Moreover, today's Jewish young adults are accustomed to life in a mixed society. Most grew up in religiously integrated neighborhoods and many were raised in households comprised of Jews and non-Jews. This trend is likely to continue as Jewish young adults generally have little regard for endogamy. Our research consistently finds low importance placed on marrying a Jew and even less on dating Jews.[7] These data are consistent with the blurring we see in the boundaries between Jewish and non-Jewish life spaces and in the diminishing appeal of the particularistic argument of the Jewish community. When we ask young Jews what is important to them as Jews, we regularly find universalistic concerns (e.g., leading a moral and ethical life) at the top of the list and particularistic ones (e.g., engaging in Jewish prayer and study) at the bottom.

American Jewish identity today is characterized by American individualism, the "sovereign self," and freedom of choice.[8] For today's young adults, "Jewish" is just one of many identities and, like the others, it moves from foreground to background as the situation dictates. The Jewish community has never been monolithic, but divisions today are not caused by splinter groups as much as by each individual designing his or her own approach to Judaism and attaching personal meaning to chosen Jewish practices.

This personalism is magnified by the fact that religious and spiritual understanding are generally very weak. People, young and old, are not doctrinaire and, indeed, they are hard pressed to articulate their beliefs, a condition common to both Jews and Americans of other faith traditions.[9] For the most part, discussion of denomination among Jewish young adults is as unsophisticated as their discussion of belief. They commonly conflate style with substance: No instruments means Conservative; a guitar means Reform. If denomination is a matter of style, then the lines among synagogues are surely blurring. Blurring is also seen in the creation of non-denominational *minyanim* on college campuses and in urban settings. Jewish summer camps often create worship services that represent a camp experience more than they do a denominational style of worship or expression of belief. Community day schools and Hebrew high schools are also creating their own hybridized brands of *t'fillot*. All these are signs of an awakening of new creation and a lessening of the denominations' hold.

Given the above challenges, we can expect to see synagogues seeking ways to convince young adults that they need an institutional setting in which to enact their Judaism. Beyond attracting membership, the successful synagogue will discover how to maintain a strong Jewish core in its purpose, practice, and teaching, while at the same time integrating a young cohort that comes to the community without these same strengths.[10]

The Successful Synagogue of the Future

The context in which synagogues operate is changing, both at the broader societal level and within American Jewry. I have indicated here a few of the trends affecting synagogue and congregation:

Synagogue
- Shifting lay and professional roles and expectations
- Increased fund-raising needs
- High competition for talent and dollars

Congregation
- Dominant values: secularism, universalism, individualism, relativism
- Low levels of education
- Weak understanding of beliefs and ideology

The leadership of the successful synagogue of the future will understand these trends and respond proactively. Its aim will be to modernize and upgrade its synagogue operations and to revitalize the congregation. These are not set goals to be achieved with a three-year plan but are continuous efforts that define the successful synagogue.

The successful synagogue will embrace best practices in the nonprofit world and it will keep pace with these as they change. It will implement advanced systems with cutting-edge tools for budgeting, tracking donors, managing membership services, and providing accountability on all aspects of synagogue operations. It may experiment with new models of efficiency and effectiveness. For example, rather than running its own school, it might outsource education to local colleges or private vendors who can provide congregation-based educational programs. It might cooperate with other synagogues in the community, bundling program, service, and operational needs to achieve greater cost efficiency. It will raise its budget line for salaries in order to compete for the managerial talent needed to upgrade the workings of the synagogue.

The successful synagogue will take fund-raising seriously. It will figure out how to "make the case" for support and it will engage professional and lay leadership in carrying the message. And it will reset the rules and expectations for board membership. Most importantly, board meetings will no longer be dominated by committee reports of work done, but will focus largely on the future direction of the organization. The discussions suggested by this volume will be taking place in the synagogue boardroom.

The successful synagogue will respond to the shifting values of American Jewry without relinquishing its own values. For example, it may respond to pervasive personalism by offering services that suit the individual needs of its members. To do so, it might engage life coaches, educational counselors, tutors, and others to fill yet-to-be-invented positions. Importantly, the work of these service providers will be grounded in Jewish understanding and purpose. In order to maintain its own core value of community, the synagogue might reconceptualize itself not as a singular congregation that gathers together a few times a year but as a network in which members attach to and connect with their own niche group in the organization (i.e., network node) on a regular basis.

The synagogue's greatest challenge, perhaps, will be to steer the waters of particularism and universalism. Jewish organizations, most of which are no longer 100% Jewish, are expected to be sensitive to and inclusive of a diverse population. The successful synagogue will be a place where everyone, Jew and non-Jew alike, feels comfortable and at home. It will have a message that it is relevant to the concerns of its members, not just as Jews but as citizens. American Jews understand that today's problems will not be repaired by the Jews alone and that mere articulation of Jewish values is an inadequate response to social needs. The model may come from the synagogue. It may adopt the model of the Jewish advocacy organizations that have long understood the importance of supporting other groups' interests as they promote their own Jewish interests.

The successful synagogue will understand the proclivities of Jewish young adults and will invest wisely in efforts to draw the rising generation into synagogue life. In his study of 20- and 30-somethings, Wuthnow attempts to prognosticate the future of the church by considering the preferences of young adults. He finds no evidence of a preference for mini- or mega-churches but does find a desire for a sense of community. He also finds no special attraction to alternative, contemporary services, which seem to appeal more to 40-somethings than to this younger cohort. If his findings extend to young Jews, then the future synagogue will not necessarily be of a certain size nor will it necessarily be an extension of current experimentation in worship services. The successful synagogue will, however, confront the inarticulateness of belief and ideology. It will reinvent its worship, drawing material and inspiration from different denominations or from no denomination at all. And it will certainly build relationships within the congregational network that ward off what Wuthnow refers to as the "fear of sitting alone."

There are two premises underlying these predictions. One is that the movements, the educational institutions, and the philanthropists who support the work of the Jewish community will renew their efforts to make serious Jewish education a normative part of the upbringing of liberal American Jews. Our analysis makes clear that level of education growing up is a critical ingredient for adult engagement in synagogue life. The synagogues alone cannot redress the current situation.

The second premise is that rabbis will be ready to lead the synagogue into the future. In the past generation, the role of the rabbi has become more complex and the seminaries are now creating new curricula to respond to a changing world. A multiple skill set that covers the concerns of both synagogue and congregation—the organization and the people—is now mandatory for success. The new requirements are likely to affect who is attracted to rabbinical school and who of the ordained chooses pulpit positions. They will also affect what synagogues are looking for in their rabbi and how the relationship grows between the rabbi and his/her congregation.

Synagogues most certainly will change over the next generation. Their strength will reside in how they deal with the issues of synagogue and their vitality will reside in how they respond to the challenges of congregation. Success rests on the capacity of synagogue leadership to step back from daily operations in order to take a thoughtful and creative look at the future that will soon arrive.

Notes

1. L.A. Hoffman, *From Ethnic to Spiritual: A Tale of Four Generations* (1996); A.J. Karp, "Overview: The Synagogue in America—A Historical Typology," in J. Wertheimer (ed.), *The American Synagogue: A Sanctuary Transformed* (Hanover, N.H.: University Press of New England, 1987), pp. 1–34; D. Kaufman, *Shul with a Pool: The "Synagogue-center" in American Jewish History* (Hanover, N.H.: University Press of New England, 1999).

2. R. Wuthnow, *After the Baby Boomers: How Twenty- and Thirty-somethings are Shaping the Future of American Religion* (Princeton, N.J.: Princeton University Press, 2007).

3. For a discussion of the relationship of these components to synagogue growth see A.L. Sales and A. Koren, *Growing Synagogues: Lessons from the S2K Westchester Synagogues.* (Waltham, Mass.: Brandeis University, Cohen Center for Modern Jewish Studies, 2006).

4. F. Chertok, B. Phillips, and L. Saxe, *It's Not Just Who Stands Under the Chuppah: Intermarriage and Engagement* (Waltham, Mass.: Brandeis University, Steinhardt Social Research Center, May 2008).

5. A.L. Sales and L. Saxe, *Particularism in the University: Realities and Opportunities for Jewish Life on Campus* (N.Y.: The AVI CHAI Foundation, 2006).

6. B.J. Lazerwitz, A. Winter, A. Dashefsky, and E. Tabory, *Jewish Choices: American Jewish Denominationalism* (Albany, N.Y.: SUNY Press, 1998).

7. For example, see L. Saxe, C. Kadushin, S. Hecht, M.I. Rosen, B. Phillips, and S. Kelner, *Evaluating Birthright Israel: Long-term Impact and Recent Findings* (Waltham, Mass.: Brandeis University, Cohen Center for Modern Jewish Studies, November 2004).

8. R.N. Bellah, R. Madsen, W.M. Sullivan, A. Swidler, and S.M. Tipton, *Habits of the Heart: Individualism and Commitment in American Life* (Berkeley: University of California Press, 1996); T. Blanchard, "How to Think about Being Jewish in the Twenty-first Century: A New Model of Jewish Identity Construction," *Journal of Jewish Communal Service*, Vol. 78, No. 1, Fall 2002, pp. 37–45; S.M. Cohen and A.M. Eisen, *The Jew Within: Self, Family and Community in America* (Bloomington, Ind.: Indiana University Press, 2000).

9. Cohen and Eisen, ibid.; Pew Forum on Religion & Public Life, *U.S. Religious Landscape Survey* (Pew Research Center, 2008). Available at http://religions.pewforum.org/reports; C. Smith and M.L. Denton, *Soul Searching: The Religious and Spiritual Lives of American Teenagers* (Oxford: Oxford University Press, 2005).

10. For a full discussion of the argument that organizational vitality can be sustained by a dual effort to preserve core teachings and introduce innovations, see: R. Finke, "Innovative Returns to Tradition: Using Core Teachings as the Foundation for Innovative Accommodation," *Journal for the Scientific Study of Religion*, Vol. 43, No. 1, 2004, pp. 19–34.

The CCAR Journal: A Reform Jewish Quarterly
Published quarterly by the Central Conference of American Rabbis.

Volume LVI, No. 1. Issue Number: Two hundred nineteen.
Winter 2009.

STATEMENT OF PURPOSE

The CCAR Journal: A Reform Jewish Quarterly seeks to explore ideas and issues of Judaism and Jewish life, primarily—but not exclusively—from a Reform Jewish perspective. To fulfill this objective, the Journal is designed to:

1. provide a forum to reflect the thinking of informed and concerned individuals—especially Reform rabbis—on issues of consequence to the Jewish people and the Reform Movement;

2. increase awareness of developments taking place in fields of Jewish scholarship and the practical rabbinate, and to make additional contributions to these areas of study;

3. encourage creative and innovative approaches to Jewish thought and practice, based upon a thorough understanding of the traditional sources.

The views expressed in the Journal do not necessarily reflect the position of the Editorial Board or the Central Conference of American Rabbis.

The CCAR Journal: A Reform Jewish Quarterly (ISSN 1058-8760) is published quarterly by the Central Conference of American Rabbis, 355 Lexington Avenue, 18th Floor, New York, NY, 10017. Application to mail at periodical postage rates is pending at New York, NY and at additional mailing offices.

Subscriptions should be sent to CCAR Executive Offices, 355 Lexington Avenue, 18th Floor, New York, NY, 10017. Subscription rate as set by the Conference is $75 for a one-year subscription, $125 for a two-year subscription. Overseas subscribers should add $36 per year for postage. POSTMASTER: Please send address changes to The CCAR Journal: A Reform Jewish Quarterly, c/o Central Conference of American Rabbis, 355 Lexington Avenue, 18th Floor, New York, NY, 10017.

Typesetting and publishing services provided by CDL Press, P. O. Box 34454, Bethesda, MD, 20827.

The CCAR Journal: A Reform Jewish Quarterly is indexed in the *Index to Jewish Periodicals*. Articles appearing in it are listed in the *Index of Articles on Jewish Studies* (of *Kirjath Sepher*).

GUIDELINES FOR SUBMITTING MATERIAL

1. Inquiries regarding publishing in the *CCAR Journal* and submissions for possible publication (including poetry) should be sent to the editor, Rabbi Susan Laemmle, in electronic form via Laemmle@usc.edu. Should problems arise, call 323-939-4084.

2. Other than commissioned articles, submissions to the *CCAR Journal* are sent out to a member of the editorial board for anonymous, peer review. Thus submitted articles and poems should be sent to the editor with the author's name omitted. Please use MS Word format for the attachment. The message itself should contain the author's name, phone number and email address, as well as the submission's title and a 1 to 2-sentence bio.

3. Based on Reform Judaism's commitment to egalitarianism, we request that articles be written in gender-inclusive language.

4. Books for review and inquiries regarding submitting a review should be sent directly to the book review editor, Rabbi Laurence Edwards, at Laurenceedwards @sbcglobal.net.

5. The Journal publishes reference notes at the end of articles, but submissions are easier to review when notes come at the bottom of each page. If possible, keep this mind when submitting an article. Notes should conform to the following style:

> Lamm, Norman. *The Shema: Spirituality and Law in Judaism*. Philadelphia: Jewish Publication Society, 1998. **[book]**

> Hoffman, Lawrence A. "The Liturgical Message." In *Gates of Understanding*, edited by Lawrence A. Hoffman, 147–48, 162–63. New York: CCAR Press, 1977. **[chapter in a book]**

> Levy, Richard. "The God Puzzle." *Reform Judaism* 28 (Spring 2000): 18–22. **[article]**

6. If Hebrew script is used, please include an English translation. If transliteration is used, follow the guidelines abbreviated below and included more fully in the **Master Style Sheet**, available on the CCAR website at www.ccarnet.org:

"ch" for chet and chaf	"ei" for tzeirei
"f" for fei	"a" for patach and kamatz
"k" for kaf and kuf	"o" for cholam and kamatz katan
"tz" for tzadi	"u" for shuruk and kibbutz
"i" for chirik	"ai" for patach with yod
"e" for segol	

Final "h" for final hei; none for final ayin (with exceptions based on common usage): atah, Sh'ma, but Moshe.

Apostrophe for sh'va nah: b'nei, b'rit, Sh'ma; no apostrophe for sh'va nach.

Hyphen for two vowels together where necessary for correct pronunciation: ne-eman, samei-ach, but maariv, Shavuot.

No hyphen for prefixes unless necessary for correct pronunciation: babayit, HaShem, Yom HaAtzma-ut.

Do not double consonants (with exceptions based on dictionary spelling or common usage): t'filah, chayim, but tikkun, Sukkot.